STEPPING UP

STEPPING UP
A CALL TO COURAGEOUS MANHOOD
——— DENNIS RAINEY ———

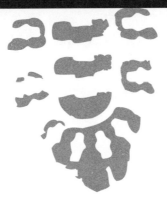

FamilyLife Publishing®

Little Rock, Arkansas

Stepping Up: A Call to Courageous Manhood
FamilyLife Publishing®
5800 Ranch Drive
Little Rock, Arkansas 72223
1-800-FL-TODAY • FamilyLife.com
FLTI, d/b/a FamilyLife®, is a ministry of Campus Crusade for Christ Inc. (known as Cru in the U.S.A).

Unless otherwise noted, Scripture quotations are taken from the New American Standard Bible®, Copyright © 1960, 1962, 1963, 1968, 1971, 1972, 1973, 1975, 1977, 1995 by The Lockman Foundation. Used by permission. (www.Lockman.org)

Names and details in some anecdotes and stories have been changed to protect the identities of the persons involved.

ISBN: 978-1-60200-231-9

FamilyLife®, FamilyLife Publishing®, Stepping Up® are registered trademarks of FLTI.

Design: Brand Navigation, LLC

Printed in the United States of America

2011—First Edition

21 20 19 18 17   1 2 3 4 5

FAMILYLIFE®

Dedicated to

Howard "Prof" Hendricks

My teacher, mentor, and friend, whose steps I've followed.

And to

Samuel Escue

James Escue

Peterson Rainey

Tyler Escue

Andrew Escue

Daniel Escue

Nathan Rainey

My grandsons, who bring great delight to my heart.

May my steps guide you, and may yours lead others

to Christ in your generation and beyond.

CONTENTS

THE FOURTH STEP: MENTOR
An Age of Investment and Impact

THE FIFTH STEP: PATRIARCH
An Age of Influence and Relevance

When I was twelve years old, I experienced a "defining moment." Don't get me wrong; it wasn't some uncommon, extraordinary experience. It wasn't a brush with death. I hadn't contracted some debilitating disease. Neither had I been traumatized by some predator. It was what my father did and what my mother stopped doing that marked me deeply for the rest of my life. And it happened in less than five minutes.

It all had to do with painting. The family who rented a property my parents owned moved out, and there was some "fixing up" and painting that needed to be done before the new tenants moved in. My father thought this would be a great project for the entire family to tackle, so on a Saturday morning, my dad, my mother, my two older sisters, and yours truly reported for duty. Mom and my sisters were working on the first floor, and my job was to help Pop paint on the second floor. And that was the problem. I never did like to paint. I didn't then, and I don't now.

So I had to somehow figure out a way to be free of what I thought was an unnecessary burden. My "ace in the hole" was my mother. Mom was always more sympathetic to her precious little boy than Dad was, and I knew that if I pressed the right buttons, she would rescue her one and only son from spending his Saturday doing something he didn't want to do. So under the guise of having to use the bathroom, I went downstairs and began to complain to Mom.

While I was in the middle of convincing my mother that I needed to take off and play with my friends, Pop showed up. As I write these words, I am vividly remembering and reliving that moment.

My mother said to my father, "Crawford, CW (my childhood nickname) is only twelve years old, and he doesn't need to be here with us all day. He needs to be enjoying himself with his friends."

Then my father said, "Sylvia, I got this. That boy one day is going to be somebody's husband and somebody's father. There are going to be people depending on him. He has got to learn how to do what he *has* to do and not what he *wants* to do."

To my mother's credit, she looked at me and then at my father, nodded in agreement, and turned away. Pop then turned to me and said, "You take yourself upstairs and paint until I tell you to stop."

And I did.

Even at twelve years old, I knew that something important had just happened. It wasn't that I had just lost a little skirmish, and this time I wasn't going to get my way. The words "somebody's husband . . . somebody's father" and "He has got to learn how to do what he *has* to do and not what he *wants* to do" kept replaying in my mind. Of course, I wasn't fully aware of the weight of what had happened. In fact, it would be years before I fully appreciated the significance of that Saturday morning. But I did have the sense that what just happened was a game changer.

My mother knew that in order for her boy to become a man, the most important man in his life needed to shape him. Pop knew that in order for his son to provide leadership and stability to those who would count on him one day, "CW" needed to embrace core lessons in manhood, obligation, and responsibility.

A transition took place that day, and I'm so glad it did. In a very real sense, it was what some would call a "rite of passage." My dad knew that in order for me not to become a fifty-year-old adolescent, I needed to make some intentional steps toward manhood. I can't tell you how grateful I am to God for the gift of Pop's courage, and that he wasn't passive when it came to my development.

Some years back when I heard my good friend Dennis Rainey give a talk that formed the outline of this book, not only did it bring to mind that Saturday morning almost fifty years ago, but it resonated deeply within me.

The message that Dennis unpacks in this compelling book is core and critical to the direction of our families, our churches, and our nation. Perhaps you think that statement is a bit overblown. I can assure you that it isn't. As a pastor, I witness daily the void and dysfunction caused by men who don't really know who and what a man is. They're not to blame. When men do not step up to and embrace the seasons of their lives, it damages hope for those who are following and limits the impact these men will have during their moment in history.

All of us need help in this journey toward authentic, intentional manhood. Thank you, Dennis, for giving us such a powerful, engaging resource that helps us and inspires us to keep moving with courage toward being the men that we can be and that indeed God has called us to be.

—CRAWFORD LORITTS

Atlanta, Georgia

ACKNOWLEDGMENTS

How can I acknowledge all the people who assisted on a book that spanned more than a decade in being written? I may not name them all, but here goes.

I want to thank Tim Grissom and Dave Boehi for sticking with me and helping *me* step up. Big time! You two are awesome men.

Dave, you have been a great sounding board for years, and this was no exception. Your DNA is in the early manuscripts, dating back to the late nineties. Thanks for not giving up and for encouraging me to "slay the beast and sling it to the public," as Churchill once said. You've been a great asset on this book and invaluable over the years in producing high-quality work that points people to Jesus Christ and changes lives. I do appreciate you!

Tim, you are the man! Thanks for your patience, counsel, coaching, encouragement, and professionalism as you worked with me. I don't think this book would have occurred had it not been for you. Thanks for your heart for seeing men step up and have the opportunity of receiving the message of this book. You are a great editor. I also want to say thanks for being a teachable man in return and for graciously responding to my challenge for you to step up—go for it!

To my friend and comrade on *FamilyLife Today*®, Bob Lepine, thank you for your steadfast belief in this project . . . all four times I attempted to write it. Your advice, counsel, and encouragement have sharpened the message of this book. Even after eighteen years, it continues to be a privilege to work with you.

I would never have been able to step away from the many demands of the office and gather my thoughts had Bill Eyster not joined the team at FamilyLife and taken a massive load off my shoulders. You are a remarkable man and a gift from God. Thank you for leading, loving, and serving the staff.

Michele Scallion gets a thousand kudos for chasing down quotes, stories, and missing documents. Your knowledge of where to find stuff that I lost was amazing! Thanks for running interference, juggling my schedule, and for just generally serving with excellence and perseverance. Please know that I appreciate you.

My assistants John Majors and Todd Nagel demand a ton of high fives. John, your help in finding stories and your heart for the message of this book were invaluable. Todd, I forgive you for being a Longhorn, but you too were a big help over the years as I worked on this book. Thanks to both of you for your servant hearts.

Rebecca Price, you are a good friend to both Barbara and me. Thank you for paving the way to make this book a reality.

Leslie Barner, you are one incredible, talented woman. Thanks for tracking a jillion details, for "owning" the production of this book, and for your eye for excellence. You are awesome!

To Steve and Elaine Crowell and Rob Tittle, thanks for being the superglue that has held the process of publishing this book together. Steve, your leadership overall has made the difference.

Thanks goes to Janet Logan and Clark Hollingsworth for being on the team and serving not only FamilyLife's constituents but also me.

To Bruce Nygren and Lawrence Kimbrough, thanks to both of you for helping me make a stab at this book a few years back and investing heavily in my life and this work.

And to the guys who read this book and gave some excellent feedback— thank you David Caranci, Fred Wood, Matt Hammitt, Matt Jenson, Michael Malloy, and Scott Hurley!

And finally to Barbara, my soul mate since 1972, the mother of our six children, and the one who shares the grandparenting load of numerous grandkids with me. You are THE BEST. I love you! Thanks for staying after me to finish the book.

WHAT DOES IT TAKE
TO BE A MAN?

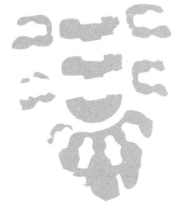

1

I CALL IT COURAGE

Courage is not the absence of fear,
but rather the judgment that something
else is more important.

—AMBROSE REDMOON

It lasted only twenty seconds, but in that short period of time, Gene "Red" Erwin embodied the courage of an ancient warrior.[1]

Gene—called "Red" by his buddies because of his wavy auburn hair— was part of an eleven-man crew on board the *City of Los Angeles*, a B-29 Superfortress. On April 12, 1945, their plane was part of a bombing raid on a Japanese chemical plant in Koriyama. One of Red's jobs was to launch white phosphorous smoke bombs to help the other planes on the raid draw a bead on and follow the *City of Los Angeles*, the lead bomber on the mission.

This was Red's eighteenth mission, so he knew the drill: open the chute, pull the pin, and release the canister. Eight seconds later, the bomb would ignite when well clear of the aircraft.

But not this time.

For some unknown reason, the first smoke bomb exploded in the drop chute, caroming back into the hull . . . back into Red's face. White-hot phosphorous, burning at 1,300 degrees, blasted smoke throughout the cabin and raised torturous havoc on Red's eyes and skin.

Red was literally on fire, and the entire crew was in danger. The smoke bomb itself was eating through the metal of the bulkhead, where the real bombs were stored. There were two options: watch the fire spread to the other munitions in the bomb bay, or crash into the ocean before everything totally blew up.

Or maybe there was a third alternative, if a man had the courage.

Grabbing the white-hot canister in his right hand, Red Erwin stumbled to the front of the aircraft, weaving blindly by instinct toward the cockpit window. Suddenly, he collided with the navigator's table that blocked his path to the cockpit. Still afire, he wedged the bomb between his forearm and rib cage, grappling with the spring latch on the table that required both hands to release and lift it. With a last surge of energy, Red scrambled into the cockpit and flung the glowing fireball through the open portal and out into the waiting waters of the Pacific. And then he collapsed in a sizzling heap.

> **EVERY MAN ON BOARD WAS SAVED, BUT RED ERWIN'S LIFE HUNG BY A THREAD.**

By the time the smoke subsided enough for the cockpit panel to become readable again, the instruments confirmed that the plane was a mere three hundred feet above the ocean's surface. A few more seconds, and any attempt to pull out of the nosedive would have been too late.

Every man on board was saved, but Red Erwin's life hung by a thread. A month after the accident, his body was still smoldering, the phosphorous reigniting from oxygen exposure each time doctors scraped another embedded fleck from his skin. He spent a solid year with his eyes sown shut and endured more than forty surgeries.

Even with a Congressional Medal of Honor hanging around his neck, he would always bear the limitations of a body seared by unimaginable heat. Yet Red Erwin would live to father four children and hold seven grandchildren in his lap. He would also coach Little League teams, follow Alabama Crimson Tide football, go to church on Sundays, and retire from a long career with the Veterans Administration.

DUTY UNDER FIRE

I've always loved stories about courage. My favorites are those about men who executed the impossible on a dangerous battlefield or accomplished great things despite obstacles and indescribable hardship—*men who did their duty under fire.*

I believe there's something in the chest of a man that responds in a unique way to stories of courage. There's a piece of every man's heart that longs to be courageous, to be bold and gutsy and etch a masculine mark of bravery on the human landscape. In our hearts, we know that a part of the core of true manhood is courage.

But many men don't realize that although most of us have not fought on a grisly, smoke-filled battlefield, all of us face battles in life that demand courage.

When you read books or watch documentaries about men who, like Red Erwin, were presented the highest award a soldier can receive—the Congressional Medal of Honor—you notice that the phrase most often repeated by these decorated warriors is "I was just doing my duty." They don't consider themselves heroes. They just did their duty in the face of danger. They were scared, but they acted anyway.

"Courage is doing what you're afraid to do," said World War I flying ace Eddie Rickenbacker. "There can be no courage unless you're scared."

Real courage is doing your duty under fire. And we all face situations throughout our lives that require that type of courage. Valor at home, protecting our wives and children. Moral courage in the marketplace. Becoming the men God created us to be, despite whatever pressures we face in the world.

STEPPING UP MEANS OWNING UP

It's never too late to step up, even when that means—especially when that means—facing our own failures and setting things right with the ones we've wounded. No one knows this better than Michael.

Married less than eighteen months, Michael was already cheating on his wife. He hadn't held high expectations when he and Angela married; he only hoped their marriage would last longer than his parents' had—seven years. But he was on course to break that record, in a bad way.

Michael knew his life was a wreck, so he decided that suicide was the way out. Only he couldn't go through with it. He made it to the bridge, and to the railing, but looking at the swirling water below, he changed his mind and went home.

But his heart hadn't changed. Soon after his near-suicide attempt, Michael announced he was going to leave. "I told Angela that I didn't want to have anything to do with her or our marriage," he says. "I just really wanted to end it."

Michael moved out, and the next time Angela saw him was when they met at the courthouse to file the divorce papers. They discovered that a paper was missing, so they didn't file for divorce that day. And then, instead of continuing with the divorce proceedings, Michael started visiting his wife at the apartment.

"We talked a lot," Angela says, "and he shared more of what he was feeling."

Michael ended the affair. Angela forgave him. They gave their marriage another try. They even moved to another city to begin a new life together. Angela was confident that her husband's infidelity would never happen again.

Sadly, she was wrong. Angela was six months pregnant when Michael confessed his second affair in two years. It had been going on for about four months. He said, again, that he wanted a divorce and that she should go live with her mom and dad.

A month or so after Angela and Michael separated for the second time, Angela's mother heard a radio advertisement for our Weekend to Remember® marriage getaway and offered to send Michael and Angela. At first Michael said he didn't want to attend. The divorce papers had already been completed. He just wasn't interested. But a few days later, after seeing the ultrasound pictures of their baby girl, Michael agreed to give it a try. The realities of fatherhood awakened something in him, calling him to stay rather than run.

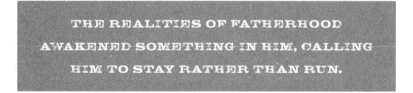

THE REALITIES OF FATHERHOOD AWAKENED SOMETHING IN HIM, CALLING HIM TO STAY RATHER THAN RUN.

At the conference, "the walls came down" for Michael. He had allowed pent-up resentment to form a barrier between himself and his wife. "I didn't understand a lot of what God's purpose was for my life," he says, "and I definitely couldn't understand what His love meant." When the speakers discussed the difference that Christ can make in a person's life, Michael recalls, "For the first time I decided to trust Jesus Christ with my life and marriage."

Michael began taking steps of courage, one after another. On the Saturday night of the conference weekend, he called Angela's parents and apologized for the poor decisions he had made and for what he had put them through. Then, several months later and after intense rebuilding of trust, he and Angela renewed their wedding vows. Sometimes it takes courage to do what's right.

Red Erwin's and Michael's stories are about courage. Both men stepped up. Red's bravery might be more obvious and celebrated, but Michael's is no less heroic. Despite his failures, Michael owned his responsibility and rescued his marriage. Asking forgiveness and becoming a responsible husband and father was a brave, bold step, and it worked.

AN INVITATION TO THE JOURNEY OF A LIFETIME

In the pages that follow, I'm going to give you a very simple yet powerful vision for what it means to be a man all the way to the finish line. I'm going to challenge you with critical decisions that every man must make during five distinct stages or "steps" of manhood. For those of you who are stuck on one of the "lower" steps, I'll share practical ways you can get unstuck and step up to the next level. And I'll talk about what every boy and young man needs from a dad, a grandfather, an uncle, a brother, or an older man.

I'm even going to talk about a sensitive subject for some of you: how a man is designed to relate to God.

Be prepared for some conflicting thoughts and emotions as you wade through this book. A friend who read an early version of this manuscript wrote to tell me that reading it "forced me to walk down four parallel paths at the same time."

The first path, he said, involved looking at his own life and his father's interactions with him. On the second path, he thought about "the man I was, the man I am, and the man I hope to be one day." The third path required examining his relationship with God. He realized where he fell short but was reminded of God's love and forgiveness.

The fourth path, he said, was the most important for him. It meant looking at the legacy he would leave behind. "What will my children say about me, my life, my purpose, and my relationship with God? The question is, am I living for me, money, or God? Do I really put Him first, or is that just religious talk?" He realized he was living too much for himself—and he was grateful to learn that lesson before it was too late.

You may find yourself digesting this book in much the same way. You will think about your own childhood, about your father, and about the good and not-so-good choices you've made over your lifetime. My hope is that by the time you finish, you will be encouraged to *step up* and be the man on your battlefield.

But you may not have as much time to prepare as you think. Your battle could be right around the corner.

Want to think about *Stepping Up* a little more or discuss it with your friends? Visit FamilyLife.com/Resources for a list of questions and talking points.

2

COURAGE IN THE VALLEY

The moment you enter the Valley of the Shadow of Death,
things change. You discover that Christianity is not
something doughy, passive, pious, and soft. . . .
The life of belief teems with thrills, boldness, danger,
shocks, reversals, triumphs, and epiphanies.

—TONY SNOW, "CANCER'S
UNEXPECTED BLESSINGS"

There are the moments and seasons in life that a man can't possibly prepare for. He is dropped into combat without warning. The greatest tests for a man come in these valleys—grim and gray times of hardship, loss, suffering, and sorrow. The birth of our thirteenth grandchild was one of those experiences.

Our daughter Rebecca, who lives in another state, went into labor at night, just as Barbara and I were going to bed. We prayed for her and went to sleep knowing that she and her husband, Jake, would contact us when the baby was born.

So when I rolled over in bed and noticed that the clock read 4:00 a.m., I thought I'd just shoot a text message off to Jake: "What's up?"

Almost instantly the reply came, "She's pushing."

At 5:45 a.m. I was awakened by another text: "It's a girl!" I smiled and went back to sleep, knowing they'd call when they were able.

There was silence for ninety minutes.

Then their call came.

We learned that after Molly was born, she didn't cry for four minutes. The doctors were suspicious of a heart murmur, and Molly had been whisked away to the neonatal intensive-care unit at the Children's Hospital in Denver. Not the news we expected.

"SOMETHING IS WRONG"

We made travel arrangements, and twelve hours later we walked into the Children's Hospital waiting area, where we were greeted by Jake. And then we heard the words, "Something is wrong with Molly's brain."

> INSTANTLY, WHAT WAS SUPPOSED TO HAVE BEEN A YOUNG COUPLE'S MOUNTAINTOP CELEBRATION OF NEW LIFE BECAME INSTEAD A FREE FALL INTO A DARK, CAVERNOUS VALLEY.

I immediately thought, *Fixing a heart is one thing. That's dangerous enough. But brain surgery? That's much more serious.*

We made our way to Molly's room, wrapped our arms around Rebecca, glanced over at Molly, and immediately began to weep. She had tubes and wires attached to seemingly every part of her body. We were stunned as we watched her tiny chest heaving, laboring to breathe. Jake was so proud of her, and he wanted to be the first to introduce us to our granddaughter.

During the next twenty-four hours, we watched helplessly as Jake and Rebecca received the news that Molly had a massive brain aneurysm. They were told that since the seventh week of development, the vein of Galen (the major vein that carries blood to the center of the brain) had delivered five times the amount of blood that a normal brain receives, and that as a result, much of Molly's brain was gone.

Instantly, what was supposed to have been a young couple's mountain-top celebration of new life became instead a free fall into a dark, cavernous valley—the valley of the shadow of death.

They weren't the only ones reeling. I had never experienced anything like this. What could prepare a man, a father, a grandfather for a crisis like this? How does a man face his own fears of inadequacy and grief, plus provide the love and comfort his family needs?

COURAGE IN THE VALLEY

I had been thrown into a battle that I didn't sign up for. I was being given a duty as a man that I hadn't anticipated. In the process of stepping into this pain-filled valley, I was about to discover a different kind of courage. There were moments when I had more questions and fears than courage. How does a man step up and lead appropriately as he watches the hearts of the ones he loves the most shatter?

Fortunately I was joined by another man—Jake's father, Bill Mutz. Bill is a good man and has been married to Pam since 1977. They had been through the valley before when he and Pam lost their firstborn son, seven-month-old Jonathan, who drowned in a bathtub.

One day at a time, Bill and I did our duty. Some were the mundane duties of getting lunch, running errands, calling family and friends, and picking up family members at the airport. Other moments were anything but routine. Molly's seven-day life was marked by the most unimaginable, freeze-framed snapshots we could ever conceive. Like sitting in a cold conference room with our wives and watching Jake and Rebecca receive the news from doctors that Molly would likely die quickly if taken off life support. That she would require fifteen to twenty life-threatening surgeries, and even if through some miraculous means she survived, she would be blind. Molly would never speak. She would likely never hear, never walk, never . . . The descriptions crushed hearts and hope.

As Bill would later recall, "One of the most difficult things for me as a man and father was remaining silent as Rebecca and Jake weighed their grim choices. It was their decision, not mine." Both of us learned that it takes courage to be silent.

THE FINAL DAY

Those seven days of Molly's life were the most challenging moments of my life. Nothing comes close. Buckets of tears. Holding my wife, daughter, and Jake while they sobbed. And as unimaginable as it sounds, there were occasions when weeping and laughter mingled.

The last day of Molly's earthly life was unforgettable.

Around noon, Rebecca and Jake honored all of us as grandparents by giving us the privilege of holding Molly and saying good-bye. None of us expected we'd get that treat. We didn't want to rob them of one moment with their precious daughter.

Barbara was first. It was quite a maneuver to make sure all the wires and tubes that were supporting Molly's life didn't get tangled, but finally there she was in her arms. Barbara kept saying how much of an honor it was hold this little princess of the King. She held her close and cooed words of love and admiration over her beautiful face. Holding back tears was impossible.

Jake's parents soaked in all of her they could. When it was Bill's turn, he stroked her face, tenderly whispered his love for her, and shared his favorite scriptures with her. Pam beamed as she gently rocked Molly and sang "Jesus Loves Me" to her. Both Bill and Pam just held her, kissing her face, holding her little hands, and weeping as they said good-bye.

As Molly was placed in my arms, she felt so warm, just like every other newborn. I tried to sing to her, and I doubt that she recognized "Jesus Loves Me" as I choked out a few words through tears.

Jake, who was videotaping, asked me, "Papa, why don't you tell Molly a story . . . one of your 'Speck People' stories?" These are adventure stories of tiny little people and equally tiny little creatures who live in a make-believe, microscopic world, facing any number of challenges that demand courage and faith. Our kids were enthralled with these tiny-people stories, and now I am telling them to my grandkids. The stories always take the Speck People to the very edge of danger . . . and then I close by saying, "And you'll have to wait until tomorrow night to hear the rest of the story."

I responded to Jake, "You aren't going to ask me to do that after I've just blubbered my way through a simple song like "Jesus Loves Me," are you?" Jake was joined by Rebecca in saying a resounding yes—they wouldn't let me off the hook.

So Rebecca and Barbara surrounded me as I held little Molly, looked into her face, and began my story: "A Speck grandfather and his Speck granddaughter went fishing for tiny Speck fish . . ." My story was less than sixty seconds long, and when I looked up into Rebecca's face, she had the biggest grin, dimples and all. She was loving the moment.

As I concluded my story, I told Molly, "The Speck grandfather and granddaughter took their fish and ate them, and then they encountered something you would never expect or believe . . . and you will have to wait until I get to heaven to hear the rest of the story."

At this point I was sobbing, but I got the words out . . . and Rebecca and

Jake started laughing. Rebecca's laughter has always been contagious, and I, too, began to really laugh.

One other detail of importance is that all of us had been gingerly holding Molly, afraid that the stress of handling her might be more than her little body could take. So as I began laughing, Jake and I looked at the heart and oxygen monitor to see if it was stressing her system, but the opposite was happening. Her oxygen saturation, which had been at 80 percent, shot up to 92 percent, and then 94, 97, 98, 99 . . . We just kept laughing, and her oxygen level climbed to 100 percent, a level it hadn't reached in twenty-four hours. All four of us cheered for Molly.

It was a moment of sheer delight and mystery. A small thing, perhaps? Yes, no doubt. But at the entrance to the valley of the shadow of death, God gave us laughter.

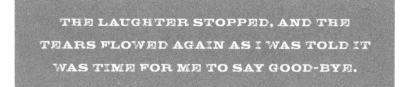

THE LAUGHTER STOPPED, AND THE TEARS FLOWED AGAIN AS I WAS TOLD IT WAS TIME FOR ME TO SAY GOOD-BYE.

Christians are the only people who can laugh in the midst of such a crisis without despair—we know where we are headed. Heaven is certain because of what Jesus Christ did for us through His death for our sins. Because He lives, we who believe and place our personal trust in Him have the hope of life after death. If a man places faith in Christ for forgiveness of his sins and surrenders his life to the Lord, then he can be certain of heaven too. It's the ultimate reason why death is different for a true follower of Christ. And it's why we could laugh as our beloved Molly was about to leave us.

The laughter stopped, and the tears flowed again as I was told it was time for me to say good-bye. Rebecca was now holding Molly. Barbara and I knelt beside her as I read her a good-bye letter:

Mighty Molly

I just met you—I feel cheated.

I don't want to say good-bye.

I know I'll likely see you in a couple of decades or so—in light
    of eternity, it won't be long, really.

Still I don't want to say good-bye.

You will always be my Molly, my granddaughter.

I'm really sad that I won't be getting to spoil you

with a doll, or go sneak chocolate,

or take you on ice-cream dates,

and eat chocolate pie and pudding.

Laughing all the time at what your mommy and daddy would say
    if they knew what we were doing.

I don't want to say good-bye.

Your seven days sure brought a lot of joy to your mom and dad's
    faces. I've watched them drink you in with their eyes, kiss you
    from head to foot, stroke and caress you.

Your parents loved you well—God couldn't have given you better
    parents. Courageous parents.

They have loved you with a sacrificial love that only a very few little
    girls like you ever get to experience.

Because it hurts their hearts so much,

oh, how I really don't want to say good-bye.

And so, sweet Molly, until that day in heaven

when we will celebrate the greatness of our God together,

(then we will go sneak chocolate and go on an ice-cream date)

I MUST say good-bye.

Good-bye, Molly Ann.

I love you, Papa.

Reflecting back on those emotion-packed, ever-so-short seven days, I now realize I learned a lot about being a man and stepping up in the valley. Without trying to explain every point, I'd like to summarize the lessons from my journey.

- In order for a man to be courageous, he must know the truth about who God is. Courage that overcomes fear comes from convictions, and convictions about life and death come from the truth of Scripture.
- The easiest thing for a man to do in a devastating crisis is to move into denial and do nothing.
- Another good man standing alongside you will help you be courageous when journeying through the valley. Bill Mutz was that man in my valley.
- It takes repeated acts of courage for a man to truly face and process his emotions. The natural tendency is to run away from them or deny they exist or to think you will be less of a man because you sob uncontrollably. Pleasure and pain were both meant to be experienced by men. For me, that took courage.
- It takes repeated acts of courage for a man to give others freedom to process their emotions differently from him and not be at the same place he is.
- A man is no less courageous if faced with a situation that he can't fix and about which he doesn't know what to do, but cries out to God in prayer, "Help me, God!"
- A man can have doubts and still step up.
- A man doesn't have to understand all of God's purposes to step up and be His man.

A number of years ago, Barbara and I were vacationing in southwest England and stumbled upon the little town of Saint Buryan, a crossroad in the country with a pub, a decaying church, and a graveyard. We stopped and read a few of the gravestones. One that was barely legible commemorated a family that lived in the 1600s. Buried beneath the stone were the mother, who gave birth to a son and died just ten days later at the age of twenty-four; her son, who lived thirteen months; and the father, who died a few days later at age twenty-five.

The faded words on that weathered limestone grave marker moved us so deeply that today they are etched on Molly's headstone:

> *We cannot, Lord, Thy purpose see*
> *But all is well that's done by Thee.*

A man doesn't have to understand God's purposes to be God's man, if he knows who God is and trusts Him.

Want to think about *Stepping Up* a little more or discuss it with your friends? Visit FamilyLife.com/Resources for a list of questions and talking points.

TIME TO STEP UP

The calling of every man is to offer
stability to a world of chaos.

—STU WEBER

A few years ago, I was sitting at dinner with about eight other men who had invited me to their duck-hunting club. Everything about the lodge oozed with rustic manhood. Thick four-foot logs blazed and snapped in the fireplace. Above the massive mantle, a half-dozen mounted mallards were "cupped," ready for landing in a watery thicket. The meal set before us was—what else?—meaty, succulent servings of waterfowl. A glance in any direction revealed a whole roomful of boots, belt buckles, and boisterous laughter.

The group at our table, like most of the others, consisted of guys who didn't know each other. Many hadn't met before this night. So the conversation, not unexpectedly, gravitated toward thoughts on the next day's hunt to highlights of previous exploits, embellished with all kinds of noises and sweeping arm gestures, the stories growing bigger with the telling.

Sure, there was some male bonding going on. We were partners in forks and knives, soon to be shotguns and hunting vests. And though the conversation was a little more interesting than everyday talk, it was still exactly what you'd have predicted. Bring any bunch of guys into this same setting, and the only difference would be in the details. Different faces talking the same stuff.

Maybe it's because I'm in my sixties and can get away with it, or maybe it's because I've heard all of this before, but I've found that as I grow older, I tire of disposable small talk much more easily. So after asking permission of our host, I popped out with a question I knew would change the tone around the table. It's a question I love asking men: *What's the most courageous thing you've ever done?*

When a man pulls back the veneer and asks a penetrating question like this, an awkward silence can suddenly descend, sucking the words right out of the room. Men's brains sort of catch and hang up. You can almost see them spinning and searching, trying to process. And yet I've discovered that even though the responses are often slow in coming, it's a question men truly love to answer.

> THE MAN WHO CLAIMS HE'S
> NEVER DONE ANYTHING
> COURAGEOUS DOESN'T UNDERSTAND
> WHAT COURAGE REALLY IS.

I've heard stirring stories of men doing their duty at key points in their lives. Being faithful to their wives when nobody was looking. Giving up pornography and confessing to their wives. Tackling difficult issues with their children. Doing what is right in the workplace, even when it's not convenient or profitable.

Many men have told about conquering their fears to step up and square their relationships with their fathers: looking a father in the eyes and forgiving him, honoring a father who didn't always deserve it, disagreeing with a father on a major decision, and standing their ground.

And yes, I've heard some phenomenal stories of war—heroic soldiers who grabbed grenades in midair and threw them back at the enemy!

I've determined that the man who claims he's never done anything courageous doesn't understand what courage really is—or how often he faces decisions that require courage.

It takes courage to step up.

FIVE STEPS OF A MAN'S JOURNEY

A number of years ago, I was asked to give a "man-up" wheel alignment to a group of 125 guys. A number had been acting like teenagers, and I was asked by the leadership of the organization that they were part of to call them to step up to their responsibilities as men.

I spoke to these men about the five stages of a man's journey through life—boyhood, adolescence, manhood, mentor, and patriarch—and his responsibilities at each stage. Sensing that these men needed a visual illustration of my message, I decided to talk about the first stage—boyhood—while standing on the first step of the stairs that led upward to a platform behind me. As I continued through my message, I moved up a step when I described each new stage.

As I spoke I could tell that the men were really connecting with this concept of stepping up. By the time I finished my message with a challenge to continue leaving a legacy even during the final stage of life, I found myself standing on the top step. Without having planned it, I'd given these men a simple visual illustration and vision for being a man.

The group morphed before my eyes. Slouching men were now sitting up straight. Heads up. Jaws set. Chests out. Somehow these good guys were being encouraged to become better men. Courageous men.

In the remainder of this book, I will talk more about these five stages of manhood. Each step offers its own set of challenges and opportunities, but one thing remains the same: no matter where you are in life, God calls you to do your duty, sometimes under fire. He calls you to courageously set aside any obstacle—your fears, your insecurities, your selfishness and sin—and step up to fulfill the responsibilities He has given you.

A NORTH STAR

As I've studied the subject of manhood over the past three decades, I've looked for the very finest definitions of true manhood. If a man is going to step up to manhood, he needs to understand what he's stepping up to be and do.

Two of my favorite definitions offer men a "North Star" to navigate through life. The first is from my friend Robert Lewis, founder of Men's Fraternity, a modern-day men's movement being used in thousands of churches, businesses, and prisons. Robert provides a working definition of *manhood* as the foundation for his curriculum: "A real man rejects passivity, accepts responsibility, leads courageously, and expects God's greater reward."

The other definition comes from pastor and author John Piper: "At the heart of mature masculinity is a sense of benevolent responsibility to lead, provide for, and protect women in ways appropriate to man's differing relationships."[1]

Note that each writer emphasizes that a real man is active in fulfilling his responsibilities. Initiative is at the heart of manhood.

That's why I talk about stepping up to your responsibilities as a man. When you step up, you assume responsibility for your family and for the assignment God has given you. It means you are an initiator, setting aside whatever inhibits you and passionately seizing your assignment.

AT ITS CORE, PASSIVITY IS COWARDICE.

What's the opposite of stepping up? Standing still . . . lying down . . . becoming a couch potato. Male passivity is a disease that robs a man of his purpose while it destroys marriages, ruins families, and spoils legacies. A passive man doesn't engage; he retreats. He neglects personal responsibility. At its core, passivity is cowardice.

Interesting, isn't it, that we don't talk much about cowards? No man wants to be labeled a coward. Instead, we instinctively value and appreciate men who seize the moment and take action—men who step up to responsibility and inspire others in the process. We cheer the quarterback who leads his team to a comeback in the fourth quarter, the firefighter or police officer who rescues others at his own peril, the businessman who elevates integrity over profit, and the dad who takes a stand and protects his family.

MANLY MEN

In the days that followed the terrorist attacks of September 11, 2001, I was impressed by the stories of courageous men who ran toward those burning twin towers and risked or sacrificed their lives to help others. Peggy Noonan nailed it in her piece for the *Wall Street Journal* when she wrote that "men are back":

> A certain style of manliness is once again being honored and
> celebrated in our country since Sept. 11. . . . I am speaking of
> masculine men, men who push things and pull things and haul

things and build things, men who charge up the stairs in a hundred pounds of gear and tell everyone else where to go to be safe. Men who are welders, who do construction, men who are cops and firemen. They are all of them, one way or another, the men who put the fire out, the men who are digging the rubble out, and the men who will build whatever takes its place.

And their style is back in style. We are experiencing a new respect for their old-fashioned masculinity, a new respect for physical courage, for strength and for the willingness to use both for the good of others.

You didn't have to be a fireman to be one of the manly men of Sept. 11. Those businessmen on flight 93, which was supposed to hit Washington, the businessmen who didn't live by their hands or their backs but who found out what was happening to their country, said goodbye to the people they loved, snapped the cell phone shut and said, "Let's roll." Those were tough men, the ones who forced that plane down in Pennsylvania. They were tough, brave guys.[2]

Those days didn't last long, but for a time, men were revered and honored for being manly. We had been attacked, and men did what men do: They protected and defended, and they took on the enemy. They enlisted. They fought. Many gave their lives.

Bob Peterson, my father-in-law and a World War II veteran who earned a Purple Heart, wanted to go fight the enemy. Even at age eighty he said, "I wish I could reenlist and go fight for my country."

SEIZE THE MOMENT

Men today are realizing that another crisis is upon us. There are no bullets or bombs, but we are on a battlefield all the same. It's a fight for our families and our future. And for this fight we need men who are willing to bravely step up and be the tough, courageous men God has designed them to be.

Winston Churchill is often quoted as saying, "There comes into the life of every man a task for which he and he alone is uniquely suited. What a shame if that moment finds him either unwilling or unprepared for that which would become his finest hour."

Every man has a task for which he is uniquely suited. You may have already discovered this—or you may be yearning for purpose or direction. Whether you are a young man or are nearing the end of your life, my charge to you is this: press into the battle, fill your lungs with smoke from the front lines, and finish strong. Be prepared to shine when presented with your finest hour.

Want to think about *Stepping Up* a little more or discuss it with your friends? Visit FamilyLife.com/Resources for a list of questions and talking points.

4

WHAT ROBS MEN OF COURAGE?

Most of our obstacles would melt away if,
instead of cowering before them, we should make
up our minds to walk boldly through them.

—ORISON SWETT MARDEN

In 2003, Hurricane Isabel slammed into the East Coast of the United States, lashing North Carolina and Virginia, then moving northward all the way to Canada, leaving sixteen dead and cutting power to six million homes. The edges of the hurricane passed through Washington, DC, prompting the president and members of Congress to find safer quarters.

That was not the case at Arlington National Cemetery, where guards have relentlessly stood vigil at the Tomb of the Unknowns every hour of every day since July 1, 1937. When the hurricane hit, the soldiers remained at their posts even though they were given permission to seek shelter.[1]

That's what a soldier does. He acknowledges the storm, but he doesn't give in to it. He stands firm.

As a friend told me, "If these men can stand guard over the dead, how much more important is it that I stand guard over the living—my wife and children?"

Like these soldiers, we are called to stand and do our duty while staring down the very storms that seek to rob us of courage, taunting and tempting us to neglect our duty and abandon our posts. These storms are packing some power. Are you ready for them?

STORM NO. 1: DAMNABLE TRAINING BY FATHERS

I once met a man who grew up in a remote section of our country. He admitted that the only advice he received as a boy from his father about women was

> Get 'em young.
> Treat 'em rough.
> Tell 'em nothing.

I wonder how that advice worked for him in his marriage.

You could say this is a legacy of the "strong, silent, tough man" image often passed down from father to son. This is the type of misguided training in manhood that has corrupted so many men as the leaders in their homes—selfish men who control their wives and children so that their own needs are met.

And that's just one part of the problem. Many boys grow up with fathers who are distant and passive. Fathers who rarely engage their families, and when they do, their half-hearted attempts to train their sons may promote irresponsible, or even immoral, behavior. Like the father whose idea of sex education for his twelve-year-old son was to take him to a strip joint. There they sat for three hours as the women did their thing onstage. No words were spoken. When they arrived home later that night, the dad told his wife, "There, I did it! Now I'm going to bed."

Another son told me about the knock at his door as he packed to go to college. His father handed him a small paper bag with this sage advice, "Don't be foolish son—use 'em."

You could likely tell your own story of how you were trained or abandoned by your father. Too many men today were raised by fathers who didn't step up to their responsibilities. Is it any wonder we have a generation of men who feel lost and aimless, not knowing how to face their fears or think rightly about themselves, women, and their own passions?

STORM NO. 2: FATHERLESS FAMILIES

The relentless, howling winds of a culture of divorce have uprooted the family tree, and with it at least two generations of men. With our high divorce rates and the increasing number of births to single women (nearly four out of ten children are born to an unwed mother[2]), the number of children in the United States who live in a single-parent household has more than doubled since 1978.[3]

> THE GREATEST PREDICTOR OF A CHILD DROPPING OUT OF HIGH SCHOOL, COMMITTING A CRIME, AND GOING TO PRISON IS A HOME WITHOUT A DAD.

Children are the innocent victims of this raging storm. The bottom line: dad is AWOL in far too many homes today. This phenomenon has prompted David Blankenhorn, founder of the Institute for American Values, to pronounce that the fatherless family "is a social invention of the most daring and untested design. It represents a radical departure from virtually all of human history and experience."[4]

The social implications of fatherless families are endless. For example, the greatest predictor of a child dropping out of high school, committing a crime, and going to prison is a home without a dad. Many young people grow up today in areas where the only adult male role models they know are live-in boyfriends or gang leaders. The fallout has only just begun: a crop of weak young men and frustrated women who are looking for real men.

One of the greatest challenges any boy could endure is trying to become a man without a father to show him how. How can a boy know what it looks like to behave as a man, love like a man, and be a man in the battle if the main man in his life has abandoned him?

My friend Crawford Loritts works with young men to build their skills as leaders. He writes that the issue of courage keeps coming up in their conversations:

> Many of [these young men] grapple with fear. . . . I think that the dismantling of our families over the past fifty years or so has almost institutionalized fear and uncertainty. Divorce, the rise of single-parent households, and the tragic assortment of abuse and dysfunction in our families have produced a generation with many young people who are afraid of risk, and afraid to make mistakes.
>
> So many of our young men grew up in homes in which they had limited or no contact with their fathers, or they had dads who were detached and didn't provide any meaningful leadership. We are left with a legacy of men who in varying degrees have been feminized. They are uncertain about who and what a man is, and how a man acts and behaves. They are fearful of assuming responsibility and taking the initiative in charting direction.[5]

My son came home one weekend from his university—a large southern school not exactly known for being the center for liberal thought—and shared with me that he had been taught in class that there weren't two sexes but five: male, female, homosexual male, homosexual female, and transgender. No wonder young men are confused and young women are left wondering where the real men are! We're living in a multiple-choice culture: are you an A, B, C, D, or E? Male sexuality and identity have become a bewildering array of options.

Think of what it must be like for young boys growing up today. Media outlets and educational elites attack the traditional roles of men and claim that a man who seeks to be a leader in his family is actually oppressing his wife and children. Our culture is permeated with sexuality, where children are exposed to explicit messages and distorted images at a far younger age than their parents were. The educational system doesn't seem to know how to teach boys, and as a result, girls are leaping ahead in test scores, college enrollment, and graduation rates. Boys are increasingly medicated because their parents don't know how to channel their masculinity, adventure, and drive.

Is it any wonder that boys grow up so confused?

"I DON'T KNOW HOW TO DO FAMILY"

In the wake of these storms lies a generation of men who don't know how to be men. They don't know how to have real relationships—with women, with their children, or with other men. And many grow up with what I call a courage deficit—they have little idea what courage looks like in a man, or what types of courageous choices they need to make as they move through their lives.

One of these men came to my front door one Saturday morning. I'll never forget him standing sheepishly in the doorway. "Mr. Rainey, in the past couple of years, I've gotten married and had two children," he said, "and I've determined that I don't know how to do marriage. And I don't know how to do family. Could you help me?"

This young man articulated what millions of young men are feeling today—inadequate, fearful, angry, and in desperate need of manhood training and vision.

STEPPING UP

The Bible tells many stories of good men behaving badly—single men, married men, and fathers gone mild or gone wild through compromise, lust, murder, jealousy, anger, passivity, or cowardice. Scripture paints men as they really are, hiding none of their blemishes or barbaric ways. The honesty of Scripture is one of the reasons I knew that the Bible would be the place to go to learn what a real man should be and do. I began looking through the Scriptures, focusing on passages that talk about men and manhood, and along the way, I discovered five prevailing themes.

1. A man controls his emotions and passions. Whether single or married, a real man tames his passions. He doesn't abuse women and children; he protects them. He keeps his hands off a woman who is not his wife, and he treats his wife with love, respect, and dignity. He keeps his eyes off pornographic images. He protects a single woman's virginity and innocence. He's not a jerk defined by his exploits below the waist. He's a man with a heart, head, and conscience.

2. A man provides for his family. First Timothy 5:8 exhorts us, "But if anyone does not provide for his own, and especially for those of his household, he has denied the faith and is worse than an unbeliever." These are strident words. When a man doesn't work and provide for his family, he feels a sense of shame. His self-worth sinks. A man who doesn't work, who can't keep a job, who moves from job to job, or who refuses to assume his responsibility creates insecurity in his wife and children. Every man needs to provide for his family.

I find that most men feel a natural sense of responsibility in this area, but many don't seem to understand that providing for their family means more than meeting physical needs. It also means taking responsibility to provide for emotional and spiritual needs. A father should train his children and prepare them to become responsible adults who know how to negotiate the swift and sometimes evil currents of culture.

3. A man protects his family. To borrow an illustration from John Piper and Wayne Grudem on the essence of masculinity: When you are lying in bed with your wife, and you hear the sound of a window being opened in your kitchen at 3:00 a.m., do you shake her awake and say, "The last time this occurred, I was the one who took our baseball bat and investigated to see if someone was breaking into our house. Now it's your turn, sweetheart. Here's the bat!"?[6]

No! That's when the man gets up.

But being a protector calls for more than ensuring physical safety. Proverbs 4:10–15 describes a father who protects his son by passing on wisdom, helping him build godly character, and teaching him to reject the lies and temptations of the world. This father is protecting not only his son but the generations to follow as the wisdom he shares gets passed on and on.

4. A man serves and leads his family. Those two words—*serve* and *lead*—may seem like a contradiction, but they are inseparable according to Scripture.

While the apostle Paul tells us in Ephesians 5:23 that "the husband is the head of the wife," he quickly puts to rest any notions that this leadership allows any form of selfish male dominance. He completes the sentence with "as Christ also is the head of the church." Then the passage goes on to say that husbands should love their wives "just as Christ also loved the church and gave Himself up for her" (verse 25).

This paints a picture of leadership that is contrary to how the world views it. A man is called to be a servant-leader—to take responsibility for his wife and children and to put their needs ahead of his own. He is called to demonstrate selfless, sacrificial love—the type of love we see in God toward His children.

5. A man follows God's design for true masculinity. Micah 6:8 tells us, "He has told you, O man, what is good; and what does the Lord require of you but to do justice, to love kindness, and to walk humbly with your God?"

The core of a man's life should be his relationship with God. The man who walks humbly with God is motivated and empowered to step up and assume the difficult responsibilities that come his way.

You see, a courageous man is never off duty.

Want to think about *Stepping Up* a little more or discuss it with your friends? Visit FamilyLife.com/Resources for a list of questions and talking points.

THE FIRST STEP:
BOYHOOD

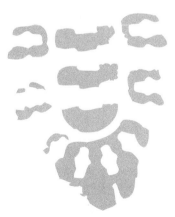

An Age of Exploration
and Discovery

"THAT BEAR'S GOING TO MAUL MY SON!"

By profession I am a soldier and take pride in that fact. But I
am prouder—infinitely prouder—to be a father. A soldier
destroys in order to build; the father only builds, never destroys.
The one has the potentiality of death; the other embodies
creation and life. And while the hordes of death are mighty,
the battalions of life are mightier still.

—GENERAL DOUGLAS MACARTHUR

They were high in the Absaroka mountain range of northwestern Wyoming in an area accessible only by horseback.[1] It was gorgeous country—one of the true remote wilderness areas of America. Pine trees, meadows, lakes, and craggy, towering mountains. Plenty of elk and plenty of grizzlies.

The two men—father and son—loved to hunt in this area. Just the two of them—far from civilization. Ron Leming Sr. had learned to hunt from his father, and he in turn taught his son, Ron Jr. They returned to the area year after year to bow-hunt for elk. "We're very close," Ron Sr. said. "These trips mean everything to me."[2]

But on all their trips, Ron Jr., thirty-seven, was the only one who had harvested an elk with an arrow. "My dad has never had the experience of getting a big bull elk with a bow," observed Ron Jr., who had a few trophy elk to his name. "I really wanted him to have that."[3]

On previous days, Ron Sr. had missed a couple of opportunities to take a shot when an elk was in range. That morning he prayed, "God, guide my arrow today."[4]

Determined to give his father an opportunity to bag an elk, Ron Jr. hid uphill. He doused his camouflage with elk scent to cover up his human smell. For thirty minutes he imitated the bugling call of an elk. Finally a big bull elk answered and was making his way to confront the competition.

Ron Jr. needed to lure the elk within forty yards of his father, hiding in the brush below, to ensure a good shot. "Everything looked good: The wind was right in our faces. The elk had no idea we were there. I was sure Dad was going to get a shot."[5]

The elk moved closer and closer . . . and then suddenly bolted into the forest.

Puzzled, Ron Jr. stood up, turned around, and discovered that something else had been stalking that elk—a five-hundred-pound grizzly bear. Perhaps mistaking Ron Jr. for the elk it had been following, the beast attacked.

Ron Sr. heard his son yell and looked up to see the giant grizzly giving chase. He recalled later, "The only thing that went through my head was that bear's going to maul my son!"[6] His next thought was a fleeting picture of his boy as a baby, lying in his arms.

Instantly he stood up, aimed, and shot. Then the bear pounced on Ron Jr. The grizzly took Ron's arm in its mouth, crushing his elbow, and shook him violently. Somehow Ron Jr. broke free and began running for safety, but the bear caught him again. He punched at the bear, trying to keep the jaws away from his head. "He definitely fought for all he was worth," Ron Sr. recalled. "That kid's Ford tough."[7]

Meanwhile, Ron Sr. was trying to string another arrow, but then he saw that the bear was covering his son. With nothing else to try, he charged at the bear and began hitting the animal on the back and head with his bow.

> **THE GRIZZLY TOOK RON'S ARM IN ITS MOUTH, CRUSHING HIS ELBOW, AND SHOOK HIM VIOLENTLY.**

To his surprise, the bear released Ron Jr. and shuffled away. Then Ron Sr. noticed that the bear was limping. "Ronnie yelled for me to shoot him again, but I didn't want to make him madder than he already was, so I just watched him," he said. "From the way he was stumbling, I knew I'd hit him pretty well with the first shot."[8]

After eighty yards the bear fell dead. Ron Sr.'s arrow had barely missed his son and had, miraculously, torn the grizzly's aorta.

God had certainly guided his arrow.

"My dad pretty much saved my life there," Ron Jr. said. "That's the thing I cannot believe in this whole story. He stood there with a bow and made that shot at a charging grizzly bear. That's amazing. You could take that shot a thousand more times and never do it."[9]

Ron Jr. had some deep bites, but no major injuries. Still, that didn't stop him from going into shock. They couldn't call for help—their cell phones didn't work that far into the wilderness. And they were fifteen miles from the trailhead, which was another thirty miles from a hospital.

Somehow Ron Sr. got his son onto a horse, and they began the six-hour journey down the mountain trail. Ron Jr. ended up spending just one night at the hospital—he was a fortunate man to be in the jaws of a bear and escape with so few injuries.

Ironically, at one point during their long packhorse trip, the two men heard another bugling elk. Ron Jr. urged his father to go shoot it—he still wanted to help his dad bag an elk.

Naturally, Ron Sr. would have none of it. "I probably couldn't hit it anyway," he remarked.

"If I got off and made it chase me," Ron Jr. said with a chuckle, "I'll bet you could hit him."[10]

YOUR SON NEEDS YOU

I've bow-hunted for elk in the rugged mountains of Montana and often wondered what I would do if I were to encounter a grizzly. In that situation, I would hope that I would charge at him with the same determination as Ron Sr.

Most of us, thankfully, have never faced a threat quite as powerful as a grizzly bear. But I believe all of us are given opportunities to courageously step up for our sons.

As your son moves through the stage of boyhood, he needs you and your protection in a dangerous culture. He needs your training, teaching, and tough love. He needs you to lay aside any obstacles or fears and courageously get involved in his life.

Let's take a look at how you can engage purposefully in a boy's life.

Want to think about *Stepping Up* a little more or discuss it with your friends? Visit FamilyLife.com/Resources for a list of questions and talking points.

WHAT EVERY
BOY NEEDS

It's better to build boys than mend men.

—TRUETT CATHY,

CEO OF CHICK-FIL-A

For a number of years, I saved a single-frame cartoon drawing that showed a freckle-faced, scruffy, blond-haired boy (maybe five years old), who was barefoot, shirtless, and in cut-off jeans, walking down a dusty trail on a hot summer afternoon. That image alone captured for me what my boyhood was like. Innocent, for the most part. Easy going. A little guy kicking around in the backwoods of the Ozarks, never too far from home or from a fishing hole.

But what still brings a smile to my face is that the boy in the cartoon was carrying a pair of skinny old cats, whose tails he had tied together in a crude knot. The caption at the bottom of the cartoon read "And he was bound to acquire experience rapidly."

Boyhood is meant to be like that. A discovery around every corner, abundant adventure, and rapid growth—embedded life lessons disguised as sharp-clawed cats!

All men start there. Some men never leave.

BOYS WILL BE BOYS

Boyhood is about exploration. A boy has license to wander and roam. But boyhood is also a time when he finds barbed wire at the top of fences and learns that some folks really mean it when they post No Trespassing signs. Boys bump into boundaries and experience the consequences for right and wrong choices.

The apostle Paul understood that boys will be boys when he wrote in 1 Corinthians 13:11: "When I was a child, I used to speak like a child, think like a child, reason like a child; when I became a man, I did away with childish things." Or, in my words:

> When I was a boy, I was all boy. I used to speak like a boy, think like a boy, reason like a boy. (All of which explains why I behaved like a boy.) But when I began stepping up, I did away with boyhood stuff.

One of the tragedies of our day is that too many boys are growing up without the guidance of a father, or another man, to show them what it looks like to do away with that boyhood stuff. As a result, they often move into adolescence and then adulthood looking like men but still speaking, reasoning, and behaving like boys.

In a cover story titled "The Trouble with Boys," *Newsweek* magazine examined the growing achievement gap between boys and girls today. "By almost every benchmark, boys across the nation and in every demographic group are falling behind," wrote Peg Tyre. "In elementary school, boys are two times more likely than girls to be diagnosed with learning disabilities and twice as likely to be placed in special-education classes. High-school boys are losing ground to girls on standardized writing tests."[1] According to the American Council on Education, young men now represent only 43 percent of college undergraduates, with women comprising nearly 60 percent.[2]

> ONE OF THE TRAGEDIES OF OUR DAY IS THAT TOO MANY BOYS ARE GROWING UP WITHOUT THE GUIDANCE OF A FATHER, OR ANOTHER MAN, TO SHOW THEM WHAT IT LOOKS LIKE TO DO AWAY WITH THAT BOYHOOD STUFF.

After examining how educators are working to close the gender gap, the article finally focused on what I'd consider the key issue:

> One of the most reliable predictors of whether a boy will succeed or fail in high school rests on a single question: *does he have a man in his life to look up to?* Too often, the answer is no. High rates of divorce and single motherhood have created a generation of fatherless boys. In every kind of neighborhood, rich or poor, an increasing number of boys—now a startling 40 percent—are being raised without their biological dads.[3] (emphasis added)

Making the problem even larger is the number of boys growing up with fathers who are physically present but emotionally distant and uninvolved.

One of the biggest needs in our generation is for men to step into the lives of boys to train them, equip them, and cheer them on to grow up as they begin the process of "manning up." And I'm not just talking about

---

fathers getting involved with their sons. I'm also talking about a generation of boys who are growing up with no male figure in their lives—boys who are desperate for a man to show them how to be a man.

WANTED: A GPS

Men don't like being lost, and we hate asking for directions. But we love gadgets, and that's why we love mobile devices that have a global positioning system (GPS).

A number of years ago, I was deer hunting. It was overcast, I was deep in a dense thicket in the woods, and there were no landmarks to help me get my bearing. As an avid hunter and outdoorsman, I was proud that I had never been lost. In fact, I couldn't understand how any *real man* could get lost. But after a couple of hours of walking in circles, I came to three very humbling conclusions: (1) If I went in the wrong direction, there was nothing but forest for twenty miles; (2) the sun was going down, and it was going to get dark and cold; and (3) I really was lost!

Fortunately I stopped going in circles, and another couple of hours later, just before dark, I stumbled out onto a road not far from my truck. But if I had carried a GPS device with me, I could have plotted a course and avoided a healthy dose of humiliation.

When Barbara and I started having children, I didn't want to admit it, but I was lost in the thick woods of parenting. I discovered that raising children involved more than potty training, settling sibling squabbles, controlling temper tantrums, assigning chores, teaching manners, and playing in the yard. With six young children, I needed a reliable guidance system, and I found it in the Scriptures. I decided to dedicate a full year of studying the Bible, discovering the irreducible essence of what children need from parents.

I found that there are four building blocks for raising children: character, relationships, identity, and mission. Every child needs teaching, training, and modeling in each of these areas.

Building Block No. 1: Character—"What Is Wise and What Is Foolish?"

I define *true character* as "response-ability"—the ability to respond rightly to authority and to the challenges we face in life.

A boy doesn't know it yet, but life is hammered out on the anvil of his choices. The problem is that wisdom does not come naturally to boys. As the book of Proverbs tells us, "Foolishness is bound up in the heart of a child" (22:15). If a boy is going to step up in life, he needs an older man who will model a lifestyle of wisdom and charge him with becoming a man of character, making right choices, and acting responsibly. A boy needs to know how to choose what is right (wisdom) and not what is wrong (foolishness).

Building Block No. 2: Relationships—"How Do I Love Others?"

When asked what the "greatest commandment" was, in essence Jesus said, "Life is about relationships with God and others" (see Matthew 22:37–40). A boy needs to know how to build authentic relationships—how to communicate and speak respectfully, how to forgive and ask for forgiveness, and how to control his natural selfishness. He needs to be trained in how to love other imperfect human beings.

Many of these lessons will be learned in the laboratory of his home, as he gains understanding in how to relate to God, his parents, and his siblings. He needs to know that if he doesn't have relationships, he misses life.

Building Block No. 3: Identity—"Who Am I?"

Every person is born with a unique identity that has its origins in God. Genesis 1:27 declares, "God created man in His own image, in the image of

---

God He created him; male and female He created them." A boy can never fully determine who he is unless he understands that he is made in the image of God—with a body, soul, and spirit.

> **BOYS GET THEIR FIRST GLIMPSE OF THEIR HEAVENLY FATHER BY WATCHING THEIR EARTHLY FATHERS.**

A boy's identity involves his "spiritual address"—his relationship with God. He needs to understand that there is a God who governs the world. As he grows up, he will be tempted to become self-focused and self-absorbed. He can begin to think that he is the very center of the universe and may be less likely to look outside of himself for meaning and purpose. A boy needs to realize that as God's creation, he is accountable to God for his life and how he lives it.

Boys get their first glimpse of their heavenly Father by watching their earthly fathers. In essence, God has given fathers the assignment of saying, "Welcome, son. As imperfect as I may be, it is my desire to take the next couple of decades and introduce you to God." If you are a father, this is *your* assignment. This is *your* privilege. No other man on the planet has the same responsibility for your son.

A boy also needs help as he grows up in this culture to answer questions such as, What is my sexual identity? What does it mean to be a boy and not a girl? He needs to have his budding masculinity affirmed and embraced as he grows up. In short, it's not just "okay" to be a boy. It's good. Very good.

A boy needs to understand that he also possesses emotions that are part of his identity. From the very start, at birth, his security—and ultimately his stability—depends on the love (or lack of love) he receives from his parents. The emotional support, affirmation, and affection he sees demonstrated *between* his dad and mom are as important as anything they teach him.

Building Block No. 4: Mission—"Why Am I Here?"

Every boy, every person, needs a reason to live—a purpose that provides meaning and impact. The apostle Paul wrote, "For we are His [God's] workmanship, created in Christ Jesus for good works, which God prepared beforehand so that we would walk in them" (Ephesians 2:10). Boys need to begin to grapple with their mission in life. And they will get the first glimpse of what having a mission looks like from their dads.

For many men, their primary mission in life is to build a successful career, provide for their families, and retire comfortably. That is what drives them, and that is the vision they pass on to their sons. But I think there is a much greater, nobler mission to pass on to boys. One of my favorite passages about children in the Scriptures is found in Psalm 127: "Like arrows in the hand of a warrior, so are the children of one's youth. How blessed is the man whose quiver is full of them" (verses 4–5).

This is powerful imagery. Think about what an arrow is created to do. Was it designed to stay in the quiver, comfortable and protected? No, it was made to be aimed and shot by a warrior at a target, to deliver a blow in battle.

Can you see the connection? Boys need to understand that they are not here on earth just to achieve worldly success and comfort. They're here to strike a blow against evil, to make a mark on their world. Just like you. After all, dads are arrows too.

LOST BOYS CAN BECOME LOST MEN

These four foundational elements represent the DNA of life. If a young boy misses just one, he can miss life as God intended it.

Think of the men you know who struggle and can't quite put life together, and see if a big part of their problem can be traced to some misguided or missing perspective in one or more of these four areas. They don't yet know who they are as men or who they want to be. They have no spiritual address and wander aimlessly. They don't know how to love and sustain a meaningful relationship with a woman or with a male friend, and they are lonely. They don't know how to make good value judgments or how to keep their promises, and they are foolish. And they just don't have a real purpose for their lives. They never seem to "nail it." They're drifting, dreaming, shifting, hoping—they never experience what God wants to do through their lives. And that is a wasted life.

I've found that many of these men never had a father or an important male figure in their lives. We're paying the price in our culture for this lost generation of boys. It's time for us to deal with our own disappointments, lay aside our guilt and regrets, and reach down and help a boy "step up."

Want to think about *Stepping Up* a little more or discuss it with your friends? Visit FamilyLife.com/Resources for a list of questions and talking points.

7

STEPPING UP AS A DAD

Build me a son, O Lord, who will be strong enough to know when he is weak, and brave enough to face himself when he is afraid; one who will be proud and unbending in honest defeat, and humble and gentle in victory.

Build me a son whose wishbone will not be where his backbone should be; a son who will know Thee—and that to know himself is the foundation stone of knowledge.

Lead him I pray, not in the path of ease and comfort, but under the stress and spur of difficulties and challenge. Here let him learn to stand up in the storm; here let him learn compassion for those who fail.

Build me a son whose heart will be clear, whose goal will be high; a son who will master himself before he seeks to master other men; one who will learn to laugh, yet never forget how to weep; one who will reach into the future, yet never forget the past.

And after all these things are his, add, I pray, enough of a sense of humor, so that he may always be serious, yet never take himself too seriously. Give him humility, so that he may always remember the simplicity of true greatness, the open mind of true wisdom, the meekness of true strength.

Then, I, his father, will dare to whisper, "I have not lived in vain."

—GENERAL DOUGLAS MACARTHUR,

"A FATHER'S PRAYER"

A few years ago, my son Ben and I had the opportunity to go to a World Series game in St. Louis. It was awesome to see my beloved Cardinals square off against the Detroit Tigers. The Cards won 5–0 (and went on to win the Series in five games), but the highlight from that evening's experience was when my friend Chip turned and asked my son between innings, "How would you describe your dad in one word?"

Watching Ben think for a moment, I quietly speculated about what he might say. I was hoping it would be some noble character quality like "loving" or "kind" or "forgiving."

Instead, my grown son's one-word conclusion of me was "intentional."

I sat there stunned. *Intentional?* If you'd given me a dictionary and a couple of days, I'd never have chosen that word! I looked at my son and thought, *You were number two in your class in high school, student-body president, intelligent . . . Is that the best you can do?*

Ben explained to Chip, "Dad was always purposeful about being a father—always teaching and training us. He tried not to leave anything to just happen."

Now that I've had some time to chew on it—and now that others in the family have weighed in and confirmed it—I've concluded that "intentional" is not a bad description.

I think I realized early on that raising my children was going to be my greatest contribution to a time that I would not see. As a result, I became very intentional in what Barbara and I taught them and in what I modeled to them.

Fortunately, I had a great "intentional" model of my own—Hook Rainey.

A BIG DAD IN A SMALL TOWN

Boyhood was pretty simple for me growing up in Ozark, Missouri. I think one reason it was so secure was that even though I lived in a small town, I had a big dad. Not in personality or size, but in character. Some boys never have that. I'm glad I did.

My dad was a quiet man with granite-like integrity. He lived his entire life a few miles from the log cabin where he was born. He was barely a teenager, and one of nine children, when his father deserted the family, leaving them dirt poor. All this took place in an era when abandonment was unmanly and divorce was unacceptable. Looking back on it all, I wonder how Dad figured out how to be a man. He could easily have been a victim and become bitter and angry.

> **LOOKING BACK ON IT ALL, I WONDER HOW DAD FIGURED OUT HOW TO BE A MAN. HE COULD EASILY HAVE BEEN A VICTIM AND BECOME BITTER AND ANGRY.**

Forced to grow up early, Dad took care of his mom and his brothers and sisters for a number of years. Somehow he managed to graduate from high school and scrape together enough money to start a service station.

Dad loved baseball. I learned later that he was a legendary country pitcher in those parts. A lefty, he was tagged with the nickname "Hook" because he evidently had a wicked curveball—the *only* thing about his life that was crooked. Local legend had it that the ball would blaze its way to home plate and then suddenly "fall off the table."

He was so good that he played in the St. Louis Cardinals farm-club system and pitched a game against Hall of Fame pitcher Dizzy Dean. Dad never could remember who won that game. "Hook" was just a six-foot-two strapping country boy who might have made it to the major leagues if his coach (or his dad) had protected him. Instead, he hurt his arm, and his dreams of the majors evaporated.

My dad not only had a sneaky curve ball; he also knew how to keep a secret. One day during the Depression, when his family wasn't looking, he and my mother eloped one weekend and went to the Kentucky Derby for a two-day honeymoon. And although I recall one argument they had when I was a boy, I really never questioned my dad's love and loyalty for my mom. They were married forty-four years until his death.

Dad taught me how to throw a curve, a slider, and a knuckleball. His knuckler was mystical. As the ball would glide to me, he'd laugh and say, "Count the stitches, son . . . count the stitches!" I'd chuckle with him as the ball floated and darted toward me. It was all I could do to catch that fluttering ball.

A bundle of memories of time with Dad now bring a smile to my face. Hunting deer and quail and fishing for white bass. His sixth-grade boys Sunday school class. Old Spice aftershave and Lava hand soap. And falling asleep together with his arm around me on a Saturday afternoon as we watched the "Game of the Week" on television. I can still feel the hair from his arm against my boyish cheek, and I can almost smell the propane on his hands from that morning's delivery.

As a boy I don't recall a single sermon that he ever preached to me, and yet Dad taught me life. He was a living message. Authentic. Humble. He didn't like "braggarts" or "blowhards," as he called them. He was faithful, honest, loyal, and kind. A man who took his responsibilities seriously. And I can count the curse words that ever came from his lips on one hand.

THE BIG SHOWDOWN

Dad coached our Little League baseball team, the Ozark Tigers, for three seasons. I was only ten when we played our first game against a well-seasoned group of veterans called the Early Birds. I didn't realize it then, but it was a classic David and Goliath showdown. I was starting pitcher, and I think the score was 12–0 in the *first* inning when Dad moved me to right field. The league didn't have a mercy rule, but they did have a time limit, and the game only lasted three innings. We didn't get a hit, and the final score was 22–0.

But Dad never gave up on us. He taught us the basics, and slowly he turned me into a pitcher and a bunch of country boys into a competitive team.

I have a team photo that hangs in my office to record what we accomplished. Two years later we made it to the semifinals in the play-offs ... and sure enough, our opponent was the Early Birds.

I'm sure they were licking their chops to play us again, but it wasn't quite the game they expected. (Guess who Dad put in as pitcher?) It was a competitive game that went down to the last play in the bottom of the last inning. We had a chance to win, but the Early Birds prevailed again, 3–2.

I was crushed that we lost. But now, over half a century later, I have a different view of that game. As I sit and stare at the team photo, it doesn't matter that we lost. What matters is that my dad was *in the picture*. Not just for three seasons, but for my life. He gave me a lot of gifts, but the best gift Hook Rainey ever gave me was that he never stopped believing in me.

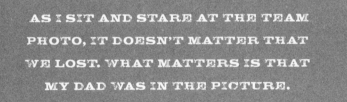

AS I SIT AND STARE AT THE TEAM PHOTO, IT DOESN'T MATTER THAT WE LOST. WHAT MATTERS IS THAT MY DAD WAS IN THE PICTURE.

When he died in 1976 at the age of sixty-six, nearly half of our town of 1,325 people came to honor him. One man, speaking of my dad's integrity, said, "I never heard a negative word about Hook Rainey."

Even now, his presence is imprinted on my life. Back in the fall of 2007, my friend Randy invited me to go bow-hunting for elk on his Montana ranch. As I started my hunt, slipping around junipers in search of a trophy, I heard the words Dad said to me many times as a boy: "Slow down, son. Slow down." Much of what I am today is because I had a father who stepped up as a man and stepped into my life as a boy.

He was more than somebody's dad. He was *my* dad.

A FATHER, A SON, AND A LIFE LESSON

Bob Helvey, one of my colleagues here at FamilyLife, tells a great story about another father who was intentional in training his son. When Bob was ten, he was a paperboy, and on one cold Virginia night, a gust of wind knocked him off his bike. Then he watched in shock as his bundle of newspapers came apart and blew away.

At that point, this boy had a choice: he could step up, be responsible, and retrieve all the papers, or he could give up and go home.

Bob did what boys do—he pedaled home.

When he arrived, his father said, "You sure finished your paper route early." Bob explained what had happened, and then his father said, "Get your coat, son, and meet me in the car."

They drove to the scene of the crime, and Bob felt some satisfaction when he didn't see any newspaper pages on the ground. But his dad parked and told Bob to follow him. They walked to a nearby house, where they were greeted by a man who invited them inside. There Bob was confronted with an amazing sight—an entire room full of newspaper pages!

With hardly a word, the two men helped the young boy piece every newspaper back together. Then Bob proceeded to complete his paper route with his father as chauffeur.

That character lesson was so powerful that Bob wrote about it forty years later in a tribute to his father. "It was a little annoying that Dad didn't give me a lecture," Bob wrote. "He knew he didn't have to. The everlasting warmth I felt of a difficult task completed, a duty fulfilled, was its own mentor."

Bob wondered how his dad had known just where to go that day. Years later he learned that after the accident, the neighbor had called his father to complain about his "good for nothing" son.

"Together they conspired to teach a young boy a lifelong lesson," Bob wrote. "It worked. The neighbor must have been a father too."

God gives us a unique opportunity as fathers to join him in what has to be one of the most noble, transcendent assignments we'll ever have as men: He gives us the privilege of joining with Him in shaping the next generation of men.

Want to think about *Stepping Up* a little more or discuss it with your friends? Visit FamilyLife.com/Resources for a list of questions and talking points.

8

YOU CAN DO IT!

A boy without a father figure is like
an explorer without a map.

—UNKNOWN

In 1923, Edgar Guest wrote about the assignment of being a boy's father. This remains one of the most profound pieces I've ever read:

I have known a number of wealthy men who were not successes as fathers. They made money rapidly; their factories were marvels of organization; their money investments were sound and made with excellent judgment, and their contributions to public service were useful and willingly made. All this took time and thought. At the finish there was a fortune on the one hand—and a worthless and dissolute son on the other. Why? Too much time spent in money-making implies too little time spent with the boy.

When these children were youngsters romping on the floor, if someone had come to any of those fathers and offered him a million dollars for his lad he would have spurned the offer and kicked the proposer out of doors. Had someone offered him ten million dollars in cash for the privilege of making a drunkard out of his son, the answer would have been the same. Had someone offered to buy from him the privilege of playing with the boy, of going on picnics and fishing trips and outings, and being with him a part of every day, he would have refused the proposition without giving it a second thought.

Yet that is exactly the bargain those men made, and which many men are still making. They are coining their lives into fortunes and automobile factories and great industries, but their boys are growing up as they may. These men probably will succeed in business; but they will be failures as fathers. To me it seems that a little less industry and a little more comradeship with the boy is more desirable.

Not so much of me in the bank, and more of me and of my best in the lad, is what I should like to have to show at the end of my career.

To be the father of a great son is what I should call success. . . . This is what I conceive my job [duty] to be.[1]

BATTLEFIELD BRAVERY

Edgar Guest clearly saw a problem that plagues many men—they know they need to step up to their responsibilities as fathers, but they are lured away by lesser achievements. They know what's right, but something holds them back.

Many of you are successfully training and developing your sons; you just need encouragement to stay in the moral and spiritual battle for your sons' souls. I also know that many of you are in need of a clear battle cry, a challenge to truly step up and courageously be the father you always wanted to become.

What's keeping you from doing your duty? Is it a fear of inadequacy? A fear of failure? Past failures? Pressure from work? Ambition? Misplaced priorities? A crisis of manhood in your own life? The desire to spend time doing what *you* want to do? An absent father when you were a boy?

Getting involved in your son's life may demand battlefield bravery as you step up to courageous manhood and fatherhood. It will mean setting aside your fears, your ambitions, and your selfish desires, and getting involved as the father you know you can be.

You can do it! Don't leave your son to find the answers to life on his own.

WHAT TYPE OF LEGACY DO YOU WANT TO LEAVE?

I think C. S. Lewis had it right when he wrote, "Courage is not simply one of the virtues, but the form of every virtue at the testing point." How well you step up as a father will determine the strength of your convictions and priorities. This is one of the most important testing points in all of life. Do you have the courage to live by your priorities?

It's time for you to decide what type of legacy you want to leave. No matter what mistakes you've made in the past, no matter what your background, no matter what your fears, it's never too late to step up and do your duty.

One of the most remarkable men I've had the privilege of interviewing for my radio broadcast *FamilyLife Today*® was John Wooden, considered by many the greatest coach in the history of college basketball. The "Wizard of Westwood" coached his UCLA teams to ten national championships between 1964 and 1975. But this is what I truly admired about the man: more than three decades after he coached his final game—and bearing down on his hundredth birthday!—John Wooden was as committed as ever to passing on a legacy to his children and grandchildren, and many of his former players. We lost a giant when Wooden passed away in 2010.

Many people don't know about the profound influence that Coach Wooden's father, Joshua, had on him. Joshua believed in building character and continually emphasized the importance of making right choices. Two of his favorite sayings, which he taught his sons, were "Never lie, never cheat, and never steal" and "Don't whine, don't complain, and don't alibi."

MORE THAN THREE DECADES AFTER HE COACHED HIS FINAL GAME—AND BEARING DOWN ON HIS HUNDREDTH BIRTHDAY!—JOHN WOODEN WAS AS COMMITTED AS EVER TO PASSING ON A LEGACY TO HIS CHILDREN AND GRANDCHILDREN, AND MANY OF HIS FORMER PLAYERS.

When John graduated from eighth grade in his small country school, Joshua gave him a card and said, "Son, try to live up to this." Eight decades later John still kept the card in his wallet and could recite these verses by heart:

Be true to yourself.

Make each day your masterpiece.

Help others.

Drink deeply from good books, especially the Good Book.

Make friendship a fine art.

Build a shelter against a rainy day.

Pray for guidance and give thanks for your blessings every day.[2]

When Coach Wooden became a father in 1936, his father gave him another poem. This poem sums up the philosophy of a man who always knew that true success came in the lives he influenced rather than in the titles he won. The poem also reminds dads that every boy needs a father who is a role model:

> A careful man I must always be;
> A little fellow follows me.
> I know I dare not go astray
> For fear he'll go the self-same way.
>
> I cannot once escape his eyes;
> Whate'er he sees me do, he tries,
> Like me, he says, he's going to be,
> This little chap who follows me.
>
> He thinks that I am good and fine;
> Believes in every word of mine.
> The base in me he must not see,
> This little chap who follows me.
>
> I must be careful as I go
> Through summer's sun and winter's snow,
> Because I am building for the years to be
> This little chap who follows me.[3]

Those are words that every father needs to keep before him. I challenge you to be involved and to be intentional with your son. Put your arm around him as he embarks on the journey of a lifetime, and courageously show him what it means to be a man.

You can do it.

A boy's life may be hanging in the balance.

Want to think about *Stepping Up* a little more or discuss it with your friends? Visit FamilyLife.com/Resources for a list of questions and talking points.

THE SECOND STEP:
ADOLESCENCE

An Age of Pushing
and Pulling

THE WILDERNESS YEARS

*Courage is going from failure to failure
without losing enthusiasm.*

—WINSTON CHURCHILL

This was an invitation Winston Churchill could not resist. He was not one to back down from a fight.[1]

Just a year earlier, in 1933, the Oxford Union voted decisively to declare that "this House will in no circumstances fight for King and Country." To Churchill, this was cowardice—"abject, squalid, and shameless."[2] It was an insult to English manhood. Didn't they know what was happening in Germany? Didn't they know how much danger England was in?

So when a group of Oxford students invited Churchill to speak, he accepted. Five hundred students showed up to hear one of the most famous men in the world. As a British officer, war correspondent, member of Parliament, and head of numerous influential government ministries, Churchill had long remained in the public eye. He was a brilliant and eloquent speaker—the kind of man who spoke his mind, even when he got in trouble for doing so.

On this evening Churchill was not among friends. When he blamed the German people for starting the Great War of 1914, "plunging the whole world into ruins,"[3] the students expressed their disapproval. He urged them to support the rearmament of Great Britain, and to his surprise the students began laughing at him. The more he tried to speak, the louder they laughed, and eventually he had to stop.

Winston Churchill is such a legendary figure today that many people would be shocked to learn that there were times when he was ridiculed and ignored by his countrymen. The fact is, he faced many wilderness experiences during his long career in English politics. Perhaps the worst was during the 1930s when he was one of the few public figures who recognized the growing threat of Adolf Hitler and Nazi Germany.

"OH, HE'S FINISHED"

During these years England was still recovering from the Great War, when nearly a million English soldiers and civilians had died. The nation was horrified as details of the senseless slaughter began to emerge, and many people became pacifists. They were determined to avoid another war at all costs.

At the same time, the world was gripped in an economic depression. Many of the English were favorably impressed by what was happening in Germany, where a fiery politician named Adolf Hitler had put his people to work and given them vision and purpose.

During these years Churchill was a member of the House of Commons, but he had few allies and almost no real power. Over and over he rose in the House chambers to warn about Nazi Germany's true goals and the danger of allowing it to build up its army and navy, but few British leaders listened to him. In a Moscow reception for a British delegation, Soviet leader Joseph Stalin asked about Churchill's political influence. Lady Nancy Astor, a member of Parliament, replied with scorn, "Churchill? Oh, he's *finished.*"[4]

Members of his own political party believed he was "reactionary and unrealistic."[5] Didn't Hitler say he wanted peace? In government offices, civil workers were warned that it was "unpatriotic to refuse to believe in the sincerity of Germany."[6]

FIGHTING DEPRESSION

Churchill definitely had his faults. He was not always a skillful politician; he was bombastic and obstinate. This made it easier for his peers to ignore him. Isolated from influential circles, he fought depression, and he struggled to stay out of debt by writing articles and books. Even that was a battle; his warnings about Germany led one newspaper—owned by a prominent pacifist—to stop paying him for columns. During these years one reporter wrote that Churchill "just looked awful. . . . If you knew he was a politician you'd think, 'He's washed out, he's had his chance and now he's through.'"[7]

> CHURCHILL NEVER GAVE IN TO THE
> PRESSURE; HE NEVER STOPPED
> TELLING THE TRUTH, EVEN WHEN
> THE NATION DIDN'T WANT TO HEAR IT.

Yet Churchill never gave in to the pressure; he never stopped telling the truth, even when the nation didn't want to hear it. Perhaps he was heartened by the fact that only Hitler seemed to take him seriously.

You could say it was Hitler who helped bring his foe back into power, because the German dictator proved every one of Churchill's warnings to be accurate. With each act of German aggression, the English people began to wake from their slumber.

When Germany invaded France in May 1940, and the British prime minister resigned in disgrace, it became obvious that the new leader had to be the man who had recognized the danger from the beginning. Appearing before the House of Commons on May 13 as the new prime minister, Winston Churchill summoned the same courage that had kept him in the fight during his years in the wilderness, and he sought to fortify the British people for the war that lay ahead:

> You ask, what is our policy? I can say: It is to wage war, by land, sea, and air, with all our might and with all the strength that God can give us; to wage war against a monstrous tyranny never surpassed in the dark and lamentable catalogue of human crime. That is our policy.
>
> You ask, what is our aim? I can answer in one word: victory. Victory at all costs, victory in spite of all terror, victory, however long and hard the road may be; for without victory, there is no survival.[8]

For years, Churchill's speeches in the House had been largely ignored. This time he received a rousing ovation.

FIGHTING BACK AGAINST PRESSURE

Churchill saw evil coming and sounded the alarm. A lesser man would have yielded to the scorn of naysayers and gone quiet. But to a wise and prudent man, silence is not an option. Not when the lives of countrymen—or loved ones—are being threatened.

> YET WHILE THE TEENAGE YEARS ARE SEEDED WITH TEMPTATIONS AND VULNERABILITIES, THEY CAN ALSO BE A TIME WHEN COURAGE IS FORGED.

Think for a moment: Do you remember what it was like to be a teenage boy? These years are a time of great vulnerability and danger for a young man. Peer pressure is unrelenting as he watches his friends choose to do things that he's not sure are right but look like a lot of fun. Life has not yet taught him that everything is not as it appears. He doesn't know that today's foolishness will be tomorrow's shame. He hasn't learned that there's no such thing as "nobody gets hurt."

Yet while the teenage years are seeded with temptations and vulnerabilities, they can also be a time when courage is forged. A teenage boy can come out on the other side of adolescence as a man, not only in body, but also in soul, if this man-in-the-making is trained by the right kind of man. A man like you. A man who recognizes the dangers in our culture and does his duty, like Churchill, despite the intense pressures he faces. The greatest pressures you will face as a father are your son's tendency to "push back" or resist your involvement and your temptation to "pull out" or disengage from his life.

Pressure no. 1: The Push Back. It's not easy to be involved in your son's life during his adolescent years. As he steps out of boyhood, he doesn't know how to become a man, and he has little experience of the lethal temptations he will confront. But his desire for independence will lead him to begin pushing you out of his life.

He will probably become more withdrawn emotionally and may talk to you less than before. He will want to spend time with his peers instead of you. He'll argue with you and stiff-arm you. He will probably think you are old-fashioned and clueless, and he'll act as though you embarrass him. He will *think* he knows more than you.

Pressure no. 2: The Pull Out. What makes the teenage years exponentially perilous is that at the same time your son and his peers are pushing back, you'll see many fathers beginning to pull out of their sons' lives. The exhaustion that comes at the end of a pressure-packed workday can result in passivity. Fathers rationalize: the easiest thing to do is disengage. And that is exactly what they do.

The antidote to the Push Back and the Pull Out is to continue *pressing in* to your son's life. As a man you must courageously step up and stay involved, wisely moving deeper into your son's life even as you are pressured to step out of it.

If you don't, you will leave your son vulnerable—standing on the step of adolescence with too many choices surrounding him, too many foolish voices influencing him, and too little maturity to make the right decisions. Without a man in his life to call him up to the next step of manhood, your son will camp out on the adolescent step as long as he can.

Want to think about *Stepping Up* a little more or discuss it with your friends? Visit FamilyLife.com/Resources for a list of questions and talking points.

10

UNDERSTANDING THE LANDSCAPE

When a boy turns 13, put him in a barrel and nail
the lid on the top. Feed him through the knothole.
When he turns 16, put a plug in the knothole!

—MARK TWAIN

If I could ask God a few questions, one would be, What did You have in mind when You created teenagers?

I'm sure my mother had the same question. There were rational reasons why she affectionately called me "Idiot Boy" when I was a teen. I *was* an idiot! Or at least I acted like one.

I blew up mailboxes with M-80 firecrackers and cherry bombs. I took a pickup from my dad's business on a joyride at 2:00 a.m., with seven of my buddies in the back. I could've killed them when I went around a corner going nearly ninety miles per hour, almost losing control.

I took a swing at my mom—and, fortunately, missed.

I raced my best friend in our dads' pickups on a gravel road, without seat belts. This resulted in my friend experiencing a rollover. He was okay, and we somehow managed to roll the truck over and get it back in its parking spot. To explain the damage, we made up an unbelievable yarn that nobody would have believed. Our parents sure didn't.

And then there was the time I stole a pound of solid sodium from the school's chemistry lab. A buddy and I went out in the country to an old bridge, and we put this gray, claylike substance into a small container and designed it so that the water could slowly seep in. If you've never witnessed what pure sodium does when it comes into contact with water, I'll have to say it really is cool, especially for a teenager. It explodes!

My buddy and I walked out on the bridge and dropped our home-made bomb in the creek below. It was a good thing that the creek was at flood stage, because the current carried the canister downstream before it blew up, creating a huge eruption and shaking the bridge. In true teenage wisdom, we both looked at each other and agreed that it might not have been a good idea to remain standing on the bridge when we released the bomb.

I'm grateful to God for all those angels He must have dispatched my way. And I am really thankful for grace, mercy, and forgiveness. I was indeed an Idiot Boy.

RAGING HORMONES

You've been a boy, and you've been a teenager. It's a confusing time. A time of raging hormones and emotional turmoil. A time of doubt, anger, and a maddening desire for independence. A time when you step back and forth between being a boy and being a man.

Remember what it was like?

- *A teenage boy's body is changing in strange and foreign ways.* He experiences weird things like erections (What's he supposed to do with that thing?) and wet dreams (What's that about?). Hair is growing in some bizarre places. Suddenly, waves of sexual desire and lust wash over him when he is near certain girls, or when he saunters by a Victoria's Secret store, or even when he looks at the swimsuit section of the J. Crew catalog.

* *He is bombarded with bewildering images, thoughts, and choices about sex and morality.* When should he begin having sex? How far is too far? Are all his friends doing it? Is it cool to experiment with bisexuality? Does having sex prove he's a man? Is it okay to look at pornography? Will he lose his mind or grow hair on the palm of his hand if he masturbates?

* *He faces relentless, unbelievable peer pressure,* with friends enticing him to join in their barbaric ways, all disguised as fun, crazy, and rule breaking.

* *He battles an emotional upheaval of anger*—and sometimes rage. At whom or what, he doesn't know. He's just angry.

* *He feels a strong gravitational pull toward independence*—to spin out of the family orbit and his parents' authority, and to prove himself.

* *He struggles with doubt and anguish and faces relentless pressure to deal with expectations*—pressures to excel in academics and make the starting team in sports and study for SATs and earn money and please his parents and impress his friends.

You know the result: a bevy of childish choices and a horde of adult consequences.

NEVER-ENDING ADOLESCENCE

Teenage boys want desperately to become men. But without training and guidance from an adult male, they will most likely take their cues on manhood from their peers and the culture. They will try to prove their manhood by indulging their lusts and fulfilling their desires. They will avoid taking responsibility and will avoid commitment in their relationships. They will make foolish choices.

Given the opportunity to go their own way, they will remain in adolescence. And they will stay there as long as they can.

Did you know that the word *teenager* didn't even exist a hundred years ago? It didn't appear in a *Webster's* dictionary until 1921. Up until the early 1900s, most of the world's population thought of people in two categories: children or adults. Because of the need for help around the home, farm, and family business, children were raised to become functioning grown-ups by the time they reached thirteen or fourteen.

> WITH EACH NEW GENERATION,
> WE HAVE LOWERED OUR
> EXPECTATIONS FOR TEENAGERS.

But with the industrial revolution, labor reform, and mandated education early in the twentieth century, a gap began to open between childhood and adulthood, leaving a space of several years to be filled in with new, imaginative possibilities.

Over the past five decades, adolescence has become a full-blown life stage and a cultural phenomenon. With each new generation, we have lowered our expectations for teenagers. Today most people in our culture believe that adolescence is a time when young men should have all kinds of freedom and fun. They are expected to rebel, experiment with risky choices, play games, look at pornography, have sex, and generally get into trouble.

We expect teenagers to continue acting like children. As Alex Harris writes in his blog *The Rebelution*, "We expect immaturity and irresponsibility" from teenagers, "and that is exactly what we get."[1]

Many observers have noted that an increasing number of young men are prolonging adolescent behavior well into their twenties and even their thirties. They cram four years of college into six or seven. Then they drift for a few more years—move back home, take a job or two that may or may not pay the bills, move in with the guys, and then move back home, and then move out again. Getting married is unthinkable; instead, they spend their evenings partying with the guys and chasing women. For many, "settling down" means leaving their hook-up culture and living with a girlfriend.

Sociologist Dr. Michael Kimmell writes of this phenomenon in his book *Guyland*. He describes Guyland as "the world in which young men live. It is both a stage of life, a liminal undefined time span between adolescence and adulthood that can often stretch for a decade or more. . . . [It's] a bunch of places where guys gather to be guys with each other, unhassled by the demands of parents, girlfriends, jobs, kids, and the other nuisances of adult life.

"In this topsy-turvy, Peter-Pan mindset," Kimmel continues, "young men shirk the responsibilities of adulthood and remain fixated on the trappings of boyhood, while the boys they still are struggle heroically to prove that they are real men despite all the evidence to the contrary."[2]

Far too many of these young men are "stuck" on the adolescent step.

A KICK IN THE BEHIND

To move through adolescence and learn how to become a man, a son needs his father's involvement. Sometimes that involvement comes in the form of encouragement; at other times, as a verbal boot in the behind.

Like the time when my oldest son, Ben, was prosecuting and persecuting his mother. He was about sixteen, and taller than she was. He was using his size and powers of persuasion to intimidate her when they argued. Arriving home one evening and finding my wife emotionally tied up in knots, I quickly determined it was time to have a little "come to Jesus" meeting with my teenage son.

We went to a local diner and ordered a couple of Cokes. (There was no way I was going to reward this kind of behavior with a burger!) I grabbed a pair of salt-and-pepper shakers and said, "Here's what's happening in your relationship with your mom. When she makes a point, you move your level of emotional intensity and persuasion one level above hers." I moved the salt shaker just ahead of the pepper. "And that causes your mom to increase *her* intensity." And I moved the pepper ahead of the salt. Then, moving the salt past the pepper once again, I said, "To which you respond and increase your intensity ahead of hers!"

I looked him straight in the eyes. "Son, relationships are life. You have to learn how to admit you're wrong. You can't just hurt people by arguing and increasing the emotional intensity."

Now *my* emotional intensity was increasing, and I gave him a warning: "You need to realize two things. First, I expect you to respect your mother. Second, I will not let you keep doing this. This is a battle you will not win. Behind your mother stands me. You will not win. Do you understand?"

That was a key moment for Ben to begin putting aside childish ways and step up. It was also a time for me to step into the life of my teenage son in a purposeful way and help develop him into a man.

We must reject the pull of our culture, which tells us to lower our expectations of our sons and let them drift through the adolescent years without any direction. They may not know it, and they may even tell us otherwise, but our sons need us in their lives. Now!

Want to think about *Stepping Up* a little more or discuss it with your friends? Visit FamilyLife.com/Resources for a list of questions and talking points.

11

WHAT EVERY TEENAGE BOY NEEDS

Whatever course you decide upon, there is always someone to tell
you that you are wrong. There are always difficulties arising
which tempt you to believe that your critics are right. To map out
a course of action and follow it to an end requires courage.

—RALPH WALDO EMERSON

When I think of what a teenage boy needs, I reflect on an incident I first described in my book *Parenting Today's Adolescent*:

The scene still causes a chill to trickle down my back.

On an outdoor stage at Mile High Stadium in Denver, Colorado, with fifty thousand men watching intensely, a fifteen-year-old boy—blindfolded and barefoot—began stepping cautiously toward a dangerous obstacle course filled with a dozen steel animal and varmint traps. All were set and ready to go off at the slightest touch of Trent's feet.

Directly in front of the boy lay the grim, gray jaws of a huge bear trap that was so powerful it could crush his leg. Several feet to the left of the bear trap lay a smaller device, a beaver trap—quick and potent.

Trent's father stood next to me, twenty-five feet away. This unusual demonstration was the closing illustration in my message. I wanted to show that children need their dads to guide them through the challenging terrain of adolescence and life. On each of the animal traps on the stage, I had fastened labels representing the "traps" of adolescence—words like *peer pressure, alcohol, drugs, sexual immorality, rebellion,* and *pornography.*

The boy took two tentative steps and was about to take a third—directly toward the bear trap—when his father, Tom, yelled into a microphone, "Trent, stop! Don't take another step. I'll be right there!" His order echoed through the cavernous stadium. Fifty thousand men sat in silence, watching.

Trent didn't take a step. He waited as his father circled the trap field and stepped in between him and the bear trap. Tom whispered instructions to Trent, then he turned his back to the boy. The young man eagerly placed his hands on his father's shoulders.

Slowly, taking small and deliberate steps, Tom maneuvered through the traps, with Trent nearly glued to his shoulders. Tom stayed as far from the traps as possible so that Trent would not bump one with his bare toes.

When the two reached me and the blindfold was pulled off, Tom and Trent hugged each other. Applause and cheering started at one end of the stadium and swelled to a thunderous, standing ovation, rolling like a tidal wave across the stadium.

Above the roar I shouted over the sound system, "Men, that's what God has called us to as fathers—to guide our children through adolescence, the most dangerous period of our children's lives!"[1]

THE SECOND STEP: ADOLESCENCE

Here's what I see happening today:

- We are providing our teenage boys with many of the skills they need to succeed at work, but we fail to prepare them to be men of their word, faithful men at home.
- They have the tools to find just about anything online, but they don't have the gear to know how to resolve a conflict with a friend or family member.
- We teach them how to drive a car, but not how to steer clear of alcohol and drugs.
- They know all the nuances of how to throw a curve or a slider and how to hit a baseball, but they are clueless about how to remain sexually pure.
- We guide them in how to get into college and make right choices in their careers, but not in how to withstand peer pressure.

Teenage young men must be trained for battle. Think of it this way: When a boy turns thirteen, you have about five years to purposefully train him for manhood. He needs to know who God is and how to relate to his Creator. He needs to know what a real man is and what he does. He needs to know how to make wise choices. And how to deal with his failures.

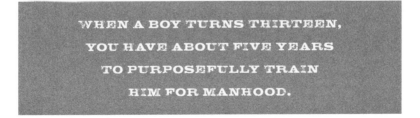

WHEN A BOY TURNS THIRTEEN,
YOU HAVE ABOUT FIVE YEARS
TO PURPOSEFULLY TRAIN
HIM FOR MANHOOD.

If we fail in this responsibility, we send our sons into battle destined to become casualties to the traps of adolescence. And ill equipped to be men who step up.

LEARNING HOW TO BE MEN

In an earlier chapter, I quoted from 1 Corinthians 13:11: "When I was a child, I used to speak like a child, think like a child, reason like a child; when I became a man, I did away with childish things."

Adolescent young men need to be trained to step away from childish things, and learn how to step up and speak like a man, think like a man, and reason like a man. Here are six nonnegotiables for training teenage young men:

1. They need help assassinating selfishness and pride. From the time a boy is born, he is full of himself. As a toddler he needs no training to become a tyrant. He does that naturally. And if allowed, he will morph from an incorrigible and bullheaded boy into a self-absorbed teen and, ultimately, a selfish adult.

Pride is "Enemy Number One" of true manhood. When a man suffers from arrogance, he isn't teachable. He can't admit fault. He refuses correction and won't be responsible. With himself as the center of his universe, all others must make their orbits around him and his needs. Ultimately he rebuffs almighty God and says, "You do Your thing and I'll do mine. I am my own god."

A man who is full of himself will never be the man God created him to be. It is only as a man understands who God is and how he relates to God as a man that he can begin the process of becoming a real man.

When a young man does understand his relationship with God, it affects all of his relationships. It makes him a giver rather than a taker. He puts the needs of others ahead of his own (Philippians 2:3–4). And he understands that a portion of his mission on earth is to help others know God personally, as he does.

Avoid feeding his primal selfishness. Instead charge him with the care and protection of his mother, his siblings, and others. Put limits on the amount of time he spends on the Internet, texting, or playing video games. Instead, put him to work. Hard work. Our sons worked ten to fifteen hours a week when they turned fourteen. Work is a powerful tool in overcoming selfishness. Sweat and calluses are good for a young man.

> WORK IS A POWERFUL TOOL IN OVER-COMING SELFISHNESS. SWEAT AND CALLUSES ARE GOOD FOR A YOUNG MAN.

Ultimately you are training your son to assume responsibility and fulfill another nonnegotiable, what Christ called the great commandments: "Love the Lord your God with all your heart, and with all your soul, and with all your mind," and "Love your neighbor as yourself" (Matthew 22:37, 39).

2. They need to learn and apply fundamental convictions and character qualities to real-life issues. What are the fundamental values and truths of your life—the lessons you want to pass on? I developed a list of more than fifty items. Here are a few:

- To know how to love, forgive, and ask for forgiveness. Too many young men know how to make a living but don't know how to resolve a conflict.
- To demonstrate common courtesies and communicate honor and respect to others, especially women.
- To know how to turn away from temptations that men face, such as lust, greed, idolatry, stealing, cheating, and lying.

- To know how to handle success and failure—some of the best lessons I taught my sons were from my failures as a father and a man.
- To know how to lead others in the valley when facing tragedy and suffering.

I wanted my sons to know that courage is ultimately built on convictions. And convictions are developed as they learn the truth about God and life, and about who they are as men. Convictions and courageous actions occur when life and truth collide. I'll never forget celebrating a courageous choice to withstand peer pressure that our son Samuel made in college. We cheered him on.

3. They need a relationship with their dad. A dad's relationship with his son is the bridge over which truckloads of truth, wisdom, training, and character lessons are driven. If the bridge doesn't exist, or if it washes out, a boy is dangerously isolated. Dads must keep that bridge in place so the supply lines can flow during the battle.

The natural tendency of teenage boys is to push their parents out while inviting peers in. To counter this, dads can map out what their sons like to do and develop common interests so they can enjoy one another and experience life together.

Relationships are built as we are transparent and authentic with our sons. Share your failures and struggles, as well as your successes with your son.

4. The best time to begin preparing a boy for adolescence is before it begins. In football, as well as in life, it's much better to be on offense rather than constantly playing defense and having a goal-line stand. One of the best things I did was to go on the "offensive" and organize a weekend getaway with my sons as they approached the teenage years. From this experience I developed a package of resources called Passport2Purity to help an adult (father, grandfather, or uncle) discuss the transformational changes that kids will experience in the teen years.

Every young man needs to know in advance about the "manhood awakening" that is so powerful it can overwhelm him. Ideally, between the ages of eleven and thirteen, or no later than fourteen, a boy needs to hear an older man talk about puberty, attraction to the opposite sex, how sex works in marriage, erections, masturbation, wet dreams, lust, and pornography. (Passport2Purity covers all of these topics in a day-and-a-half experience with your son. For more information, see ShopFamilyLife.com.)

5. *Young men need to be with men.* Young men need to talk about manly things with older men. They need to rub shoulders with men who are modeling what it means to be a man. And they need to experience ceremonies and celebrations around what it means to be a young man.

A few years ago, I helped my friend Robert Lewis, founder of Men's Fraternity, with a DVD series called Raising a Modern-Day Knight. This series is designed for fathers and sons to complete in a weekend or in six weekly sessions and contains a number of unforgettable ceremonies that commemorate a boy's passage to the next step of manhood. (For more information about this series, see ShopFamilyLife.com.)

6. *Teenage boys can't be allowed to linger in adolescence.* Like a young eaglet that gets pushed out of the nest at the appropriate time, a young man must learn to fly on his own. If the nest is too cushy, if all of his creature comforts are there for his enjoyment, then he may set up his high-definition television and perch for a while.

With both of my sons, I remember a conversation that occurred sometime around their nineteenth birthdays: "Dad, I just don't get as much money from you and Mom at college as my friends do. I can't make it on what you give me."

To which I smiled and responded, "Son, I understand. You are becoming a man. A man with adult tastes and expectations. Your mom and I love you, but you need to know that we are not committed to helping you satisfy these desires. If you want to eat out, buy things, and go places, you're going to have to earn money."

> ASK ANY SINGLE WOMAN IN HER TWENTIES AND THIRTIES, AND SHE'LL TELL YOU THAT THERE IS AN ENDANGERED SPECIES OF REAL MEN WHO WANT TO ASSUME THE RESPONSIBILITIES OF A MAN.

I am concerned about a migration of immature eagles back to the home nest. Some are delaying the manly duties not only of assuming responsibility for rent, food, and monthly bills, but also of stepping up to find a wife and begin a family. Ask any single woman in her twenties and thirties, and she'll tell you that there is an endangered species of real men who want to assume the responsibilities of a man.

DON'T GIVE UP

It's easy to become discouraged when you feel as though you keep teaching the same lessons over and over to teenage boys, and you think they'll never grow up. And then God surprises you.

Benjamin and Samuel both attended the same university, and their time overlapped a couple years. I remember speaking with a female friend of theirs, who said, "Oh, did you hear what happened at the Campus Crusade for Christ meeting on campus the other night? First of all, Benjamin stood up. He shared how he was going to take a year off from school and volunteer to go to Estonia and be a missionary to reach college students.

"After he finished, he sat down, and the next person to share was Samuel. He told everyone what a phenomenal brother he had—how much he loved him, how much he admired him, what a mentor he had been to him, what an example he had been of following Jesus Christ, and how much that meant to him as a freshman at the university. And then Samuel put his arms around his brother and just hugged him."

It was one of those moments parents dream about. These were the same boys who once argued and fought with each other so often that we wondered if they would ever become friends. I wanted to hear this story one more time!

I think God occasionally has compassion on parents and gives us just a glimpse of the men our sons are becoming. I tell this story to give you hope and to encourage you to keep on being faithful to bring up your sons "in the discipline and instruction of the Lord" (Ephesians 6:4).

At some point you will see the fruits of your efforts as these young men step up.

Want to think about *Stepping Up* a little more or discuss it with your friends? Visit FamilyLife.com/Resources for a list of questions and talking points.

12

EVERY MAN'S BATTLE

The greatest barrier to success is the fear of failure.

—SVEN GORAN ERIKSSON

Many issues are robbing men of their manhood today, but none is more widespread and detrimental than sexual immorality.

Think of what our sons are exposed to as they grow up. The culture is saturated with sexual images on television, in movies, on the Internet, on their phones—everywhere they look. Most boys see hard-core pornography by the age of ten, and many become addicted to online pornography as teenagers. It isn't a matter of wondering if they will see pornography; it's more of a question of how much they've seen and how they should respond. In thousands of ways, they are told that the mark of a real man is his sexual experience.

Is it any wonder that they grow up with a warped perspective of their

---

sexuality? That they carry those views into their twenties and thirties, and ultimately into their marriages? That their sexual experimentation eventually impacts and undermines their marriages?

I'm still not sure what caused me to ask my fourteen-year-old son the question, but one day around dinnertime I said, "I've been thinking about you recently, and I was just wondering if you've been looking at any stuff you ought not to be looking at?"

He knew exactly what I was asking. He looked at me as if I were omnipresent and said, "Well, as a matter of fact, today at lunch as I was eating my sandwich in the classroom, a couple of guys brought a *Playboy Magazine* into the room and asked me if I wanted to look at it."

I tried to be calm as I asked, "So what'd you do?"

He responded, "I wrapped up my sandwich . . . and walked out of the room!"

At that point I broke into a huge grin and shouted, "Yes!" as though my son had just scored in the Super Bowl. He had.

In our culture, we cannot afford to forsake our sons to sort through this complex issue alone. If you had to face it alone as a teenager, I'm truly sorry. You know how destructive this issue can be. I urge you to let your experiences motivate you to protect your son from those entanglements. Join him in the battle. Step into his life. Help him. To do that, you'll need to step up and out of the issues in your life that are like quicksand.

TIRED OF BEING A WIMP

Fred Stoeker, coauthor of *Every Man's Battle,* is a man who knows very well the need for fathers to guide their sons through this issue. He's also a man who learned that sometimes the most courageous thing a man can do is simply to open a door.

When his son Jasen was eleven, Fred began to think of all the changes, pressures, and temptations Jasen would face as a teenager.[1] He wanted to begin meeting regularly with his son to take him through a book on preparing for adolescence, but he worried about how Jasen would react.

For five nights in a row, Fred stood outside Jasen's bedroom door, wanting to talk with his son but unable to summon the courage. Yet Fred knew he needed to do something to help Jasen avoid the same mistakes he had made as a teenager. He remembered that his grandfather had been unfaithful as a husband. He remembered seeing his father's pornography, hidden under the bed. He remembered reading a letter his father was writing to a mistress. He remembered the time his father wanted to teach him about sex by setting him up with a prostitute.

> FOR FIVE NIGHTS IN A ROW,
> FRED STOOD OUTSIDE JASEN'S
> BEDROOM DOOR, WANTING TO
> TALK WITH HIS SON BUT UNABLE
> TO SUMMON THE COURAGE.

Despite his repeated vows not to follow in his father's footsteps, Fred couldn't live up to those ideals. At one point as a young California stockbroker, he was juggling four women, sleeping with three of them and engaged to two. Miraculously, God lifted him from his sex-infested lifestyle and eventually brought him into a relationship with a godly woman, who became his wife and settled him into the role of husband. And father.

Now, years later, Fred found himself standing outside his son's bedroom, grappling with a responsibility familiar to all dads of teenage boys— opening a father-son dialogue about sex. He didn't know exactly how to do it, but he couldn't shake the conviction that it was time to, in his words, "put a stop to this corruption in the family tree."

Finally, tired of acting like a wimp, he knocked on Jasen's door.

TALKING FROM THE HEART

After a few seconds of forced small talk, Fred realized he was doing nothing to disguise the fact to his son that he was there on serious business. So, taking a deep breath, knowing he was in too far to back down, he tossed aside his fears and just started talking. Straight. From the heart.

"Look, son, you're entering a time of life when things are going to start being different. Your body will be changing. Your friends will be having more influence on you. You'll start noticing girls in a different way. It's just going to be totally new."

"I know, Dad. It's called *per*verty, right?"

Fred laughed. "Well, no, it's called 'puberty' actually!"

He went on to say that it would be a little hard to understand sometimes. He didn't want Jasen to figure this thing out all by himself, or to piece it together from what he heard from his friends. He wanted to begin meeting to talk about it together and read the Bible together and pray for God to help him handle what was ahead.

Fred expected Jasen to roll his eyes and mutter, "Yeah, sure, whatever." So he was shocked to hear his son say, "Dad, I really think it's a good time for us to be going through this. . . . I've been scared lately."

"Son, what are you scared of?"

"Well, I've been having a tough time saying no to my friends lately, and I don't understand it, and I've just been scared that I can't say no."

Tears came to Jasen's eyes, and Fred saw that his son really needed him. That began a new chapter in their relationship, as Fred began helping Jasen understand how to trust God through the issues he faced during adolescence.

Fred wonders what would have happened if he had never gone into Jasen's room that night. He thinks Jasen would have been left to face "perverty" on his own—just as Fred had done so many years before.[2]

As fathers we face many moments like the one Fred experienced standing in the hallway outside his son's bedroom. Moments that call for "twenty heroic seconds" (Remember Red Erwin's story from chapter 1?) when we must set aside our fears and step up and step in.

This is the courage required on the hidden battlefield of the home. Without this courage, we abandon our sons to fight alone.

Do you want that happening on your watch?

Want to think about *Stepping Up* a little more or discuss it with your friends? Visit FamilyLife.com/Resources for a list of questions and talking points.

THE THIRD STEP:
MANHOOD

An Age of Stepping
Up Again and Again

13

A MAN OF
ENDURANCE

Optimism is true moral courage.

—ERNEST SHACKLETON

The voyage seemed mad.[1] A desperate gamble. Row a twenty-two-foot lifeboat through Antarctic winter seas, through gale-force winds and swells over fifty feet high to a tiny island eight hundred miles away? In 1916, with only a compass and a sextant to guide them? And no Under Armor, Gore-Tex, or goose-down gloves.

Hopeless? Without a doubt!

Yet Ernest Shackleton knew that he and his companions had no choice. They were stuck on Elephant Island, a barren pile of rocks that was swept each day by wind and snow. Nobody in the outside world knew that he and the twenty-seven men on his expedition were even alive. Nobody was looking for them. So he devised an impossible and desperate plan to reach the whaling communities on the island of South Georgia and then send back a boat to rescue the men left on Elephant Island. It was their only hope.

By this point, Shackleton and his men on the Imperial Trans-Antarctic Expedition had already experienced enough adventure for a lifetime. A forty-year-old veteran of two previous Antarctic trips, Shackleton had raised funds in England for his quest to be the first to cross the South Pole by land.

Their ship, the *Endurance*, steamed out of South Georgia on December 5, 1914—summer in Antarctica. The plan was to travel to a harbor a thousand miles away and then begin the land portion of their expedition. But ice floes in the Antarctic seas were unusually heavy for summertime. Shackleton and company made it within eighty-five miles of their destination, but then, after only forty-five days at sea, the *Endurance* was frozen fast in pack ice.

For three weeks they tried to break free, and then they finally realized they were stuck until spring, seven months away. To come so close was "more than tantalizing; it was maddening," wrote ship surgeon Alexander Macklin in his diary. "Shackleton at this time showed one of his sparks of real greatness. He did not rage at all, or show outwardly the slightest sign of disappointment; he told us simply and calmly that we must winter in the Pack, explained its dangers and possibilities; never lost his optimism, and prepared for Winter."[2]

> FOR THREE WEEKS THEY TRIED TO BREAK FREE, AND THEN THEY FINALLY REALIZED THEY WERE STUCK UNTIL SPRING, SEVEN MONTHS AWAY.

The next few months went surprisingly well, despite arctic storms and temperatures down to thirty degrees below zero. In May the sun disappeared and didn't rise again for four months. Shackleton put the men on a set daily work routine and organized games, dog races, sing-alongs, and book discussions. He participated in all the activities, trying to keep the men's spirits up and their hope alive.

Events turned against them again in October. When the ice pack began to melt, the *Endurance,* made of the hardest wood known to man at that time—ironwood—was hopelessly wedged between shifting ice floes, and eventually was crushed from the pressure. For the next few months, the men camped on ice floes, hoping they would drift toward an island where supplies were stored. Then on April 9, 1916, the ice became dangerous—cracks would open up without warning under their tents, and several men nearly lost their lives.

They boarded the lifeboats they had pulled from the *Endurance* and rowed for seven days on a harrowing journey through subzero temperatures, surrounded by a pod of killer whales that terrified the men with their "blood-curdling" blasts. Finally, exhausted and frostbitten, they arrived at Elephant Island. It was the first time they had stood on solid ground in 497 days.

BATTLING WIND AND WAVES

Shackleton was a man of action, and he knew the morale and physical condition of his men was deteriorating. "Shackleton sitting still and doing nothing wasn't Shackleton at all," Macklin wrote. Only fifteen days after landing at Elephant Island, he and five others shoved off in a lifeboat. They had only four weeks of food and water onboard. If they didn't make South Georgia island in that time, Shackleton said, "We were sure to go under."[3]

The seas and the weather were every bit as bad as they had feared. Snow and heavy winds. Giant waves that tossed the small ship about like a toy. The men constantly pumped water out of the lifeboat, and when they could manage a nap, they often woke up thinking they were drowning.

Once, Shackleton noticed a line of clear sky. Then he realized that it was actually the crest of a giant wave. "During twenty-six years' experience of the ocean in all its moods I had not encountered a wave so gigantic," he later wrote. "It was a mighty upheaval of the ocean, a thing quite apart from the big white-capped seas that had been our tireless enemies for so many days."[4] Somehow the men endured the wave and kept the boat afloat.

Throughout this chaos, captain Frank Worsley managed to use fleeting glimpses of the sun to guide them toward South Georgia. In a twisting line, they made it closer and closer to the island. And then, just after sighting land, they were hit by the worst storm of all, a full-fledged hurricane. They battled the wind and waves nonstop for nine hours.

Finally the weather cleared enough for them to land. But there was one problem. They had landed on the wrong side of the island.

"WE HAD SEEN GOD IN HIS SPLENDOURS"

Reaching the nearest whaling colony would have required a 150-mile trip around the island. But the lifeboat was too damaged; that option was out. Shackleton announced that they would hike across South Georgia island on foot. A journey no one had ever undertaken before.

The island was nothing but mountains, crags, crevasses, and treacherous snow. Their map of the island was blank in the middle because nobody had ever penetrated more than a mile from the coast.

To Shackleton, however, it was the only option.

At first they got mixed up in the fog and headed in the wrong direction, ending up farther along the coast. They retraced their steps, and then set out across the island.

Twice they reached high points in the mountains, only to discover that huge crags of rock barred their way. On a third ascent, they made it over but then were enveloped by fog and couldn't see more than a few inches in front of them as they cautiously made their way down the mountain. As the sun set, they arrived at a huge snowfield and, knowing they lacked the clothing to spend the night at that altitude, decided to slide down in the near darkness. "We seemed to shoot into space," Worsley wrote. "For a moment my hair fairly stood on end. Then quite suddenly I felt a glow, and knew that I was grinning!"[5]

They continued through the night and then had to retrace hours of hiking when they discovered once again that they were off course. Shackleton called for a rest and then forced himself to remain awake when the others immediately fell asleep. "I realized it would be disastrous if we all slumbered together," he wrote, "for sleep under such conditions merges into death. After five minutes I shook them into consciousness again, told them that they had slept for half an hour, and gave the word for a fresh start."[6]

After thirty-six hours, the weary men stumbled into the whaling camp, the final leg of their impossible journey finally over. They looked like dirty, drunken beasts, with ragged clothes and long, tangled hair. It was nearly two and a half years since they had left the island to begin their expedition.

The rest of the men were rescued. Not a single man perished.

"In memories we were rich," Shackleton wrote later. "We had pierced the veneer of outside things. We had 'suffered, starved and triumphed, groveled down yet grasped at glory, grown bigger in the bigness of the whole.' We had seen God in His splendours, heard the text that Nature renders. We had reached the naked soul of man."[7]

ABSOLUTE DETERMINATION

Today, historians look upon Ernest Shackleton and his expedition with awe. Setting aside his disappointment when his mission failed, he threw himself

---

into leading his men to survive and to find a way back to civilization. Books have been written about his leadership and management skills.

The eight-hundred-mile journey to South Georgia island is considered one of the most remarkable sea voyages ever. And nearly forty years passed before British explorer Duncan Carse led another group in crossing the island on foot. After following much of the same route, Carse said of Shackleton, "I don't know how they did it, except they had to."[8]

Two things impress me most about Shackleton: his selfless attitude toward his men, and his courageous determination to do whatever he could to survive. He didn't let the obstacles stop him. He knew what needed to be done, and he refused to give up.

As men we are called to a similar type of courage: to know our duty, to lead our families, to pursue God's call for our lives with dogged determination, to never give up despite whatever obstacles we experience in life.

As we move out of adolescence, it is important for us to exhibit endurance as we step up to our responsibilities as real men. As I will explain in subsequent chapters, we need the courage to initiate, the courage to protect, the courage to avoid stepping backward and down into adolescence, and the courage to believe.

And one other thing before we move on. Stepping up in being a man is *not* a one-time event. It's a journey of thousands of courageous steps. And a jillion small ones. Stepping up to courageous manhood is a lifetime process.

Want to think about *Stepping Up* a little more or discuss it with your friends? Visit FamilyLife.com/Resources for a list of questions and talking points.

14

THE COURAGE TO INITIATE

Once upon a time, men wore the pants, and wore them well. Women rarely had to open doors and little old ladies never had to cross the street alone. Men took charge because that's what they did. But somewhere along the way the world decided it no longer needed men. Disco by disco, latte by foamy non-fat latte, men were stripped of their khakis and left stranded on the road between boyhood and androgyny. But today there are questions our genderless society has no answers for. The world sits idly by as cities crumble, children misbehave and those little old ladies remain on one side of the street. For the first time since bad guys, we need heroes. We need grown-ups. We need men to put down the plastic fork, step away from the salad bar, and untie the world from the tracks of complacency. It's time to get your hands dirty. It's time to answer the call of manhood. It's time to wear the pants.

—FROM AN ADVERTISEMENT
FOR DOCKERS JEANS

Initiative is the essence of manhood. Nothing comes to the man who is passive, except failure.

Men are not meant to be spectators. Real men accept responsibility rather than making excuses and look for solutions instead of casting blame. They reject the "I'm a victim, so let me off the hook" mentality and find a way to push ahead through the storm.

On the other hand, the disengaged man, whether single or married, will settle for diluted, bland maleness. Life happens to him; he doesn't happen to life. His expectations are low. And so are his achievements.

I hope you're not counting on him. I hope you're not him.

ABDICATING THEIR ROLES

Some men demonstrate more courage in their jobs than they do in their families. A friend recently made an observation about a neighbor and expressed questions about why some men don't step up at home:

Rebecca is in her late thirties and is married to Bill, a man in his early forties who is a successful CEO of the leading oil company in a Middle Eastern country. Bill was a U.S. oil-company exec when they met fifteen years ago; then they moved [to the Middle East], had children (his second family), and raised them until they started school.

Rebecca [and their children] moved back to the U.S. to get the younger son, who has ADHD issues, the right educational environment. For the past five to seven years, she's lived here, and Bill has visited about once every month or two—it seems to work for them. However, the boys are growing, now twelve and fourteen and out of control, and she can't handle the virtual single-mom thing anymore.

Finally, Bill announced last month that he's stepping down from his international gig and coming home to spend more time with the family. Everyone is excited. His twenty-two-year-old daughter by a previous marriage is posting the news to her Facebook page—"Dad's coming back!"

Sounds like he's finally agreeing to engage in the family he supports financially, right? No. Yesterday I learned that the twelve-year-old son is being shipped off to military prep school, and Dad is considering a new job in Ireland. Jaw dropping.

Why is it that some men can initiate great tasks and conquer overwhelming obstacles at work, yet remain passive in relationships or in leading at home? It's as if there's a disease that infects the male species. None of us is exempt from the passivity virus. Over the years I've done a little inventory of my life and listed some of my own lame excuses for why I haven't taken the initiative when faced with a duty or challenge:

- *Taking the initiative is hard work, and I'm tired.* I hate to admit this, but pure selfishness and laziness have been the cause of most of my passivity. In years past, after solving problems at work, I just wanted to vegetate, watch television, and not get involved with cleaning up the kitchen, helping with homework, or putting the kids to bed. And I certainly didn't want to deal with bigger issues, such as repairing a breach in my relationship with my wife or addressing a disciplinary issue with a child. On multiple occasions I've had to pry myself out of my easy chair and into situations that I would rather have ignored. Being a man will involve pain. Initiative requires sacrifice and self-denial.
- *I don't know how to initiate.* When I was single, developing a relationship with a woman was risky. The learning curve was steep,

and there was always the fear of rejection. Later, as a husband, at times I found it easier to abdicate leadership to my wife. As a dad I knew I needed to develop a relationship with my daughters and take them on dates, but what were we supposed to talk about? Other responsibilities, such as having a "birds and bees" conversation with my children, were awkward and easy to rationalize putting off until sometime in the future.

- *Taking the initiative means I might fail.* Or it may mean I've already failed, and it's easier not to risk failing again. Whether it was asking a young lady out on a date when I was single; leading my wife in planning, discussing the family budget, or hammering out boundaries and discipline for the children; or just dealing with the basics of leading my family, I found that the fear of failure creates a gravitational pull toward passivity. But real men take action. And when they do, great things can happen. Just ask my friend Tom.

THE TEN QUESTIONS

For many years, Tom Elliff and his wife, Jeannie, have taken time away from their normal routines to get away and be together. They'd have some romantic dinners and fun conversations, and generally just have a wonderful time talking about their lives.

One year Tom decided to elevate the discussion and, in the process, open himself up in a way few husbands ever do. He developed a list of questions based on issues he knew were of concern to Jeannie, and then he sprung them on her during a retreat in the Rockies:

1. What could I do to make you feel more loved?
2. What could I do to make you feel more respected?

3. What could I do to make you feel more understood?
4. What could I do to make you more secure?
5. What could I do to make you feel more confident in our future direction?
6. What attribute would you like me to develop?
7. What attribute would you like me to help *you* develop?
8. What achievement in my life would bring you the greatest joy?
9. What would indicate to you that I really desire to be more Christlike?
10. What mutual goal would you like to see us accomplish?

That type of vulnerability takes initiative and courage!

You might be thinking, *There is absolutely, positively no way I'm ever going to ask my wife questions like that.*

"I WAS ALMOST BLOWN AWAY"

When I interviewed Tom and Jeannie on my radio program *FamilyLife Today®*, I asked her how those questions made her feel. Jeannie replied that the first thing that crossed her mind was a sense of tremendous honor that her husband wanted to know how she felt about important issues in their lives. "I was almost blown away," she recalls. "It was wonderful."

Tom has reviewed these same ten questions with Jeannie many times since that first conversation. When Tom told me about this experience, I couldn't help but think it was a perfect illustration of 1 Peter 3:7, which instructs husbands, "Live with your wives in an understanding way, as with someone weaker, since she is a woman; and show her honor as a fellow heir of the grace of life."

Asking these questions, and actually listening to the answers, helps a husband understand his wife's needs. It connects them in a deeper way as a couple and makes them accountable to each other.

> **THE FIRST THING THAT CROSSED HER MIND WAS A SENSE OF TREMENDOUS HONOR THAT HER HUSBAND WANTED TO KNOW HOW SHE FELT ABOUT IMPORTANT ISSUES.**

This is the type of love, understanding, and leadership we are called to as men.

SPIRITUAL INITIATIVE—THE MOST FRIGHTENING OF ALL

Over the years I've challenged men to take the initiative and improve their marriages in another way. This action requires bedrock courage.

No, it's not initiating sex. By comparison, that's risky indeed, but nowhere nearly as challenging as . . . praying daily with your wife.

Now, some men are already praying daily with their wives. But I've seen that look of hesitation and even fear in the eyes of many men when I've given them this challenge. It's way out of their comfort zone.

I'm not certain that Barbara and I would still be married had it not been for this spiritual discipline of experiencing God together in our marriage. It has kept us from building walls in our marriage, it has forced us to forgive each other, and it has kept us focused in the same direction.

A businessman, who works for a well-known corporation, took my challenge a number of years ago. He and his wife had been married for years and had two children. At the time, he was experiencing some difficulties in his marriage—he was angry over the lack of time they spent together, both relationally and sexually; he had begun drinking (again); and they had been sleeping in separate bedrooms for two years. They were not considering divorce and remained committed to the marriage, but in his words, "We were both on different pages, spiritually and mentally. She wanted to have Bible studies together and pray, but I wasn't willing, due to my inner anger at her."

A few years later, our paths crossed again, and he wrote to tell me that when he took the initiative to pray daily with his wife, their relationship was transformed:

Over a period of time and consistently praying together, we have seen amazing changes in our lives. Quickly the level of anger subsided. Each night our prayers became easier and meant more. We seemed to move onto the same page, our attitude toward each other changed, and we began liking each other again.

We also saw changes in our parenting; we started talking more and having in-depth conversations. Over the last few years, our conversations have turned to deep, meaningful reviews of our lives and the mistakes we've made. We share hurts, frustrations, and worries. We both seem to want to help each other and support the other in times of need.

As we learned to love and respect each other, our sex life has grown into a beautiful expression of our love and is more satisfying than ever. Our walk with God has grown deeper, individually and as a couple. Our lives seem to be connected on a spiritual level as never before. As with any marriage, problems still arise, but now we feel equipped to deal with the issues in a positive way.

Jesus Christ has done a mighty work in our marriage, and we attribute much of that success to the fact that every night we approach the Throne of Grace together. It truly is His grace that has sustained us. Only He could salvage our train wreck of a marriage and not only make it survive but thrive.

Can you imagine what would happen in your marriage, in your family, if you demonstrated that type of initiative and courage? My encouragement is *try it*. If you miss a day, then pick up again tomorrow and pray together. I've found that the men who initiate prayer with their wives have a dramatically different relationship with them in less than two years.

Want to think about *Stepping Up* a little more or discuss it with your friends? Visit FamilyLife.com/Resources for a list of questions and talking points.

15

THE COURAGE TO PROTECT

Courage is almost a contradiction in terms.
It means a strong desire to live taking the form of readiness to die.

—G. K. CHESTERTON

It began as a fun shopping date with my daughter Laura, who was thirteen at the time. I never dreamed it would end the way it did.

Laura decided that she wanted to go where her older brothers and sisters went to shop: Abercrombie and Fitch. There she found a beautiful baby-blue sweater and went to the dressing room to try it on. While I was waiting I noticed a life-size poster of a young man, completely nude, leaning up against a boat dock, knee-deep in water. The shot was from behind, but I hadn't asked to see that guy chilling in his birthday suit.

I stood there looking at that poster thinking that this was a clothing store, and that image was totally inappropriate for my daughter and other girls. Finally I asked if I could please talk with the manager. The young man, who couldn't have been more than thirty, came over, and I greeted him with a smile. I shared with him that I had six children and was a good customer;

then I said very kindly, "This picture . . . I'm sorry, but it's just indecent." I thought I'd get agreement.

Instead he quipped, "I beg to differ with you, sir. By whose standards?"

A little stunned by his response, I replied with measured firmness, "By any standard of real morality."

By that time, Laura had wandered back with her sweater. I pointed to the picture of the chiseled, buff-buddy's buns, looked the manager squarely in the eyes, and said, "Sir, if that picture is not indecent, then I'd like you to drop your pants and get in a similar pose to that guy in the picture."

He looked at the picture, then at my daughter, and then back at me. He looked like a deer in the headlights. There was a moment of silence, full of anticipation. Then he shook his head and said, "Huh-uh."

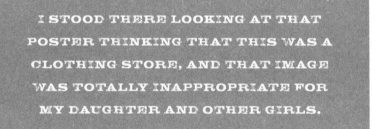

I STOOD THERE LOOKING AT THAT POSTER THINKING THAT THIS WAS A CLOTHING STORE, AND THAT IMAGE WAS TOTALLY INAPPROPRIATE FOR MY DAUGHTER AND OTHER GIRLS.

I probably shouldn't have pressed the point, but I added, "Come on, you said that picture is not indecent. Come on, drop 'em."

"Huh-uh."

I smiled and said, "You know, it's a good thing you didn't drop your pants, because you could have been arrested for indecent exposure."

Then he replied, "Well, if you think that's bad, you should see our catalog."

So I went over and opened the catalog. One photo showed four teenage girls in bed with a boy. I'm not sure what they were advertising—maybe bedsheets—because none of them had any clothes on. I pushed the catalog back and said, "I'd like you to take my name and phone number. I'd like someone from your corporate office to give me a call."

To which he politely said, "Sir, I can take your name and address, but they're not interested. They really don't care what you think."

My response was kind, but firm: "I just want you to know I'm only one customer. I'm just a daddy of six kids, but I've got a lot of friends. And I want you to know that wherever I go, I'm going to use this episode as an illustration of a company that doesn't care about the future of our young people, their morality, or the future of our nation."

I figure I've shared the story with about five million people on various radio broadcasts, at conferences, and now in this book.

REAL MEN ARE WARRIORS WHO PROTECT

What America does need is men, real men, who won't slither away from an issue or a battle.

British politician Edmund Burke gave this chilling reminder: "All that is necessary for the triumph of evil is that good men do nothing." When it comes to evil invading a man's life and marriage, his children's lives, his work, and his community, the easiest thing for him to do is nothing. We are losing the battle with evil today because far too many "good" men have done just that—nothing.

Doing nothing is like gravity; it just happens. *Nothing* is the fruit of passivity. *Nothing* is the consequence of a lack of conviction. It's the by-product of lazy leadership at home. Doing nothing expresses no risk, exerts no initiative, and experiences no reward or triumph. Doing nothing is the natural bent of most men.

The easiest thing to do is nothing.

Cowards do nothing.

One of the greatest lies of our day is that one man, one husband, or one dad can't make a difference. As a single man, you *can* protect the innocence of a single woman you are dating by being a noble man of character and keeping your hands off her. As a husband and father, you are the warrior who has been charged with the duty of pushing back against the evil that seeks to prey on your wife, daughters, and sons. Stepping up to courageous manhood starts here.

If you don't step up, who will?

COURAGE STARTS AT HOME

When I consider my responsibility to protect, I can think of many times when I failed because I didn't act with initiative and determination:

- As a single man, I didn't push back against peer pressure but instead went with the flow. I am ashamed of the evil that I encouraged or participated in.
- I didn't protect my wife, for example, from the demands and expectations of others who had no idea the load she was carrying.
- I remember the time one of our daughters came downstairs, ready for church but wearing an immodest dress. Instead of telling her to go change, I was too wimpy to engage her in what I knew would be a battle. So I said nothing.
- Another time, a teacher at school was mean-spirited to one of our children, and I allowed it to continue unreported far too long.

Failures like these, once I confronted them and confessed my passivity and irresponsibility, have made me more determined to step up and act like a man.

When you think about protecting your family, perhaps the first things that come to mind are keeping your house locked, or holding on to your child's hand on a crowded sidewalk, or investigating a strange sound downstairs in the middle of the night, or training your children what to do if the house catches on fire. But as I've looked at my responsibilities as protector at home, I've realized that they entail much more. For example:

- *I've established boundaries to protect my marriage.* I'm doing battle for my marriage when I don't meet with a woman by myself unless the door is open or there is a window so that others can observe. I don't have lunch with other women alone. I don't travel alone in a car with other women. (In the past thirty-five years, I've been in a car alone with another woman other than my wife twice.) I copy Barbara on e-mails written to women, and I don't have private conversations with women on social websites without her knowing. At the same time, I do battle for my marriage by helping Barbara with household chores, continuing to court her, taking her on dates and getaways, and spoiling her with an occasional gift.
- *I attempted to protect my children by training them in the choices they would make.* I've already mentioned the Passport2Purity weekend getaways I organized with both sons in their early teens to discuss peer pressure, dating, sex, pornography, alcohol, and more stuff the culture was throwing at them. I continued these conversations with my sons through the years—we even talked about things like dealing with aggressive girls who pursued them sexually, and what to do if they saw a fight breaking out at school. In addition, Barbara and I made a big effort to get to know our kids' friends, especially once they reached junior high, and peer pressure kicked into high gear. We wanted to be aware of the good influences and the potentially bad ones.

- *I attempted to protect my daughters by dating them and, later, by interviewing their dates.* On these dates I showed them how a young man was to take care of them, what they should expect from a guy, and how to deal with sexual overtures. I explained why it was important to dress modestly, and I discussed it before they reached the age when they began experiencing peer pressure on the issue. I met with their dates and asked each young man to keep his hands and lips off my daughter.[1]

- *I protected my family by working with Barbara to set up boundaries regarding media.* We set standards on the types of movies and television programs we would watch. We made rules about when and where our children could access the Internet, and we talked about how to protect their privacy and how to guard against sexual predators. If I were a father who still had children at home today, I'd also be setting boundaries on cell phones, texting, and video games, as well as installing porn filters on all computers.

A trained warrior also has battlefield vision that anticipates the future. He scans the horizon and assesses dangers that are coming so that he can prepare for them.

And he realizes he is never off duty.

WARRIORS IN THE COMMUNITY AND THE BOARDROOM

America not only needs warriors at home; it also needs men willing to use their influence to protect their communities, and even the nation. Like my friend Scott Ford, former CEO of Alltel, who told me of the pressure he felt from stockholders who wanted to increase the company's profits by putting pornography on the mobile phones they sold. Scott stood firm, and many times he stood alone.

Robert Rowling, whose holding company owns Omni Hotels, is another corporate warrior. He pulled all the pornography out of his hotels at a cost of more than six million dollars, reasoning that if he didn't want his son to view that stuff, why should he make it possible for other men or their sons to stumble?

I also think of John Downs, a businessman, husband, father, and grandfather who refused to do nothing when he heard that casinos were coming to his community. John not only shut them down in his town, but he also heroically stepped up and rallied other "good" men, who eliminated privately owned casinos in the state of Alabama.

The Scriptures contain a simple admonition that men of all ages need to take to heart: "Do not be overcome by evil, but overcome evil with good" (Romans 12:21). Men, we are in the midst of a cosmic conflict between good and evil. Wars are made up of battles, and battles demand men who will step up and fight.

You may never be a warrior in a corporate boardroom, but you may have the opportunity to step up in other ways. Perhaps it will be a matter of taking a stand against deceptive practices in the company where you work, speaking out against sexual harassment, or talking with your child's teacher if he or she shows an inappropriate film during class.

It takes courage for a man to step up and push back against evil. It will mean that you don't go with the flow. You can't fight every battle, but you can get involved when opportunities come your way. It may mean taking a stand for decency in your community.

When men don't step up, the cost of doing nothing means that indecency, immorality, and other aberrant behaviors become the norm in the culture. Our children and grandchildren will pay the ultimate price if we turn our heads. When men are not warriors, when men don't push back against evil with good, the evil we were meant to conquer turns around and preys upon us and our descendants (see Isaiah 59:11–15).

> WHEN MEN DON'T STEP UP, THE COST OF DOING NOTHING MEANS THAT INDECENCY, IMMORALITY, AND OTHER ABERRANT BEHAVIORS BECOME THE NORM IN THE CULTURE.

In all of these various engagements with the culture, real men are firm but gracious. Having convictions doesn't give a man the license to be rude or to pummel another person with his beliefs. Truth and love must be kept in proper tension with each other.

"FREAKING" ON THE DANCE FLOOR

I have one last admonition: Be ready! You never know when you'll come face-to-face with an issue that demands courage and stepping up.

A number of years ago, a couple of our teens attended a junior-high dance at school. Barbara and I decided we'd go and check it out. As we entered the darkened dance hall, we saw about thirty kids off in the darkest corner, doing a dance called "freaking." Now, if you haven't seen this, trust me; it's an imitation of intercourse, but with clothes on.

A handful of parents were huddled near a light in a corner watching, grumbling, and grousing about what they saw, but generally doing nothing.

I walked past the parents and stood near the swaying crowd. I watched as two boys drew a young lady in between them, literally. As I stood there deciding what to do, my palms grew clammy, sweating from anticipation. I thought, *Here I am, a forty-five-year-old man, and I'm afraid of what a couple of pimple-faced, fourteen-year-old boys think about me?* (Remember: courage is not the absence of fear but doing your duty in the face of fear.) I finally concluded, *What they're doing is absolutely indecent. It's ridiculous for me to cave in to fear!*

So I stepped into the crowd of "freaking" dancers and tapped one of the young men on the shoulder. I smiled sternly and told him to knock it off. I challenged him to treat the young lady with dignity and respect.

He had a very blank look on his face. I could see him thinking, *Whatever . . .*

His response didn't matter, because one small step had brought victory. Feeling more courageous, I approached another trio of gyrating teens and busted them up. I looked over my shoulder, and a bunch of dads were now joining me.

Here's the point, guys: God made men to pierce the darkness. He didn't make us to fight every battle, but he did make us to stand for truth, to embrace standards. And when men don't embrace convictions, they will be paralyzed and neutralized by the culture. They won't step forward and can't step up because they don't have the mandate of truth resonating in their souls. In the absence of real men pushing back against evil, the culture continues its downward spiral and becomes increasingly shameless, lewd, and vulgar.

Do not be overcome by evil. Step up and *kindly* overcome evil with good.

Want to think about *Stepping Up* a little more or discuss it with your friends? Visit FamilyLife.com/Resources for a list of questions and talking points.

16

THE COURAGE TO RESIST TEMPTATION

Cowardice asks the question, Is it safe? Expediency
asks the question, Is it politic? Vanity asks the question,
Is it popular? But conscience asks the question, Is it right?
—MARTIN LUTHER KING JR.

I've talked a lot about stepping up in this book. Yet one of the biggest problems today is men who are straddling the steps between adolescence and manhood, and sometimes step down.

You see it in the news on a regular basis—politicians, athletes, and celebrities who admit they've been cheating on their wives.

Talk to single women over the age of twenty, and they'll likely give you an earful about guys who prefer horsing around with their buddies and playing video games to developing a real relationship with a woman. I don't blame single women. I'm with them. One has to wonder if one of the most courageous things a single man will ever do is to get off the fence, say "I DO," and make a lifelong commitment to a woman.

However, straddling the steps between adolescence and manhood isn't restricted to the young or the single. You hear it in the stories of middle-aged women who talk of husbands who decided they weren't in love anymore and bolted for freedom. Husbands who succumbed to the charms of a younger woman or retreated into a cocoon of self-absorption and irresponsibility—behavior that should have ended during adolescence. In other words, these men found themselves with one foot on the manhood step as they leaned on the other foot in adolescence. They looked like men but acted like boys.

Fortunately for my friend Dan, he had a friend who stepped into his life and helped keep him from stepping down.

RECONNECTING WITH AN OLD FLAME

Dan is a man's man. A family man. Venerable. Virtuous. If you met him, you'd like him. But despite an impeccable track record, he almost threw it all away.

He was going through a season in his life when everything was difficult. He felt pressure at the church where he was the pastor, and he felt the unrelenting pressure of being a good husband and father.

It all seemed so innocent. He missed his twentieth high-school reunion, and soon afterward he received a note from an old girlfriend who had dumped him just before the prom. She said she had missed seeing him at the reunion; he was the one person she had hoped to reconnect with after all these years. Dan wrote back and said he would love to reconnect as well, and perhaps they could get together the next time he returned for a visit.

So he set up a lunch meeting for him and his wife, Kathie, to meet with this woman. Notice that Dan included Kathie. He wasn't a total fool . . . at least not yet.

When Dan's old flame walked through the doors of the restaurant, he thought to himself, *She is better looking now than she was at seventeen!* Almost involuntarily he said to Kathie, "Wow, would you look at that?" which got him a sharp elbow in the rib cage.

After a cordial lunch, Kathie left the table for a few minutes, and instantly the conversation turned more intimate until she returned. When lunch was over, they said their good-byes, and Dan thought, *Well, that was that.*

After Dan returned home, he received another note from the woman saying she had hoped they could spend more time together, just the two of them. She had some things she really wanted to talk about, and she needed some "closure" on their relationship. He wrote back and said he would be speaking at a conference in Portland that fall (one of our Weekend to Remember marriage getaways, if you can believe it!).

In her reply she said that, by "coincidence," she'd be in Portland that very weekend on business, so maybe they could get together. So they set a dinner date.

But this time Dan didn't tell Kathie.

Now, Dan is a geologist by training, a very smart man. And he did what men have been doing for centuries: he rationalized his actions. He even thought he could use the rendezvous to tell his old girlfriend about his faith in Christ!

But in his gut he knew it was wrong, and for several months he felt increasingly guilty. Every time he opened the Bible, no matter what passage he tried to study, all he could hear was God telling him, "Don't do it!" Here he was, a pastor of a growing church and the leader of a beautiful family, with a wife and three children, a man who spoke around the country on how to have a good marriage, and he was about to put himself in a situation where he might throw it all away in a single compromise.

The only thing that saved Dan from certain shipwreck was an accountability partner, a man he met for breakfast every week to talk about their lives and to challenge each other to walk in obedience to Christ. Dan called this good friend his "sparring partner."

To Dan's credit, at one of their breakfasts, he finally told his friend about what was going on. After listening, his sparring partner courageously *stepped into* Dan's life and said, "You're an idiot!"

Then he took out his cell phone and said, "You're going to call this woman right now and cancel that date."

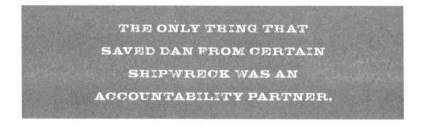

THE ONLY THING THAT SAVED DAN FROM CERTAIN SHIPWRECK WAS AN ACCOUNTABILITY PARTNER.

Dan did exactly that. He told the woman that he was happily married and that it wasn't appropriate for him to continue any sort of relationship or communication with her. He apologized for his improper attitude toward her and asked for forgiveness.

When Dan hung up, a truckload of pressure fell off his shoulders. Then that true and faithful friend said the one thing Dan didn't want to hear, the one thing that would fully prevent him from falling back toward adolescence. "Next, you need to tell Kathie all about this. And if you don't tell her by Friday, I'm going to tell her."

Dan did tell Kathie the whole story. Kathie's response was what every man needs from his wife when he admits a weakness or temptation. She said she was disappointed that he didn't trust her earlier with the problem. She admitted that she knew this woman had deeper intentions than just talking about old times. Kathie also sensed that Dan was struggling, but just knowing that his sparring partner was committed to help bring to the surface and conquer those struggles gave her security in the marriage relationship. She was proud to be married to someone who was man enough to be accountable to others.

THE POWER OF TEMPTATION

Dan almost took the bait. That's what temptation is, you know; it is a "lure" toward sin. Satan is a master angler who knows exactly where your weaknesses are. He is an expert at presenting you with bait that is designed perfectly for you.

Temptation isn't sin; it's when we swallow it and act on it that it becomes sin. And it can destroy our lives.

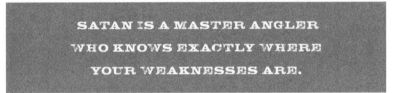

SATAN IS A MASTER ANGLER WHO KNOWS EXACTLY WHERE YOUR WEAKNESSES ARE.

You may not think it takes much courage to face your temptations, but it does. Accountability is a proactive step toward never underestimating the power of temptation. Manhood requires us to resolutely "flee from youthful lusts and pursue righteousness, faith, love and peace, with those who call on the Lord from a pure heart" (2 Timothy 2:22). We have to put the lure of adolescence behind us, face upward, and keep stepping up through our lifetime.

Temptation never ceases as we grow older. One friend approached me after listening to me speak on this topic and admitted, "I'm sixty years old, and over the past couple of weeks, I've found myself standing on the adolescent step. I can't believe I'm sixty and still struggling with these issues."

I can.

We're all just one very slippery step away from stepping down. One foolish choice made in a moment of weakness can wipe out years of integrity.

You and I can become idiots very quickly!

Want to think about *Stepping Up* a little more or discuss it with your friends? Visit FamilyLife.com/Resources for a list of questions and talking points.

17

THE COURAGE
TO BELIEVE

Men lust, but they know not what for; they wander,
and lose track of the goal; they fight and compete, but they forget
the prize; they spread seed, but spurn the seasons of growth;
they chase power and glory, but miss the meaning of life.

—GEORGE GILDER, *Men and Marriage*

When I was twenty, I made a wonderful discovery: before I could step up to true manhood, I had to decide what I truly believed. I was a junior in college when I finally answered the spiritual wake-up call that had been gnawing at me.

My first two years in college were a contrast of human failure and success. I nearly flunked out during my freshman year and nearly made straight As my sophomore year. I didn't make the traveling squad on the basketball team my freshman year, and as a sophomore I started the last game that if we'd won would have put us in the hunt for the national championship game for junior colleges. I was turned down for dates as a freshman, and I had plenty as a sophomore. As a freshman I was pretty much of a loser, but during my second year, I served as president of the student body and had achieved everything I'd dreamed of to that point.

But my life was empty. Purposeless. I was depressed and even thought about suicide. But in the end, I loved myself too much to do that.

I sensed that I needed to step up to something, but what?

Spiritually speaking I had treated Jesus Christ like a spare tire, pulling Him out of the trunk in an emergency and then putting Him back in after the crisis was over.

Despite my arrogance and emptiness, during the summer of 1968, between my sophomore and junior years, the "Hound of Heaven" chased me down with His love, and I surrendered as completely as I knew how. God used a man, Alan, to call me out of a self-centered existence into a relationship with Jesus Christ that enabled me to experience the rich design that God had created for me as a man.

> SPIRITUALLY SPEAKING I HAD
> TREATED JESUS CHRIST
> LIKE A SPARE TIRE.

Alan opened the Bible and taught me out of the book of Romans. He showed me from Scripture that God's love for me remained the same whether I loved Him or not. The love of God, demonstrated in the person of Jesus Christ, slowly turned my heart toward Him.

I realized that Jesus Christ didn't come to be a spare tire. He didn't come to be a hitchhiker or even a passenger in the front seat. He came to be the Driver and Master of my life.

That summer I did a scary thing, a courageous thing. I peeled my fingers off the steering wheel and relinquished total control of my life to Him as Savior, Lord, and Redeemer of my life. The decision to trust Christ completely redirected my life and secured my eternal destiny.

SETTING ASIDE MY DOUBTS

My junior year in college became an adventure. No longer was life lived on just a physical plane; God was at work in me, changing me and giving me a noble mission of representing Him. Then I met another man who also called me to step up—Tom Skinner.

Tom was the chaplain of the Washington Redskins and came to campus to give a series of messages. I had the privilege of driving Tom to his speaking engagements, and we became friends.

Although I've forgotten most of what we talked about, I do recall Tom beginning and ending each of his five messages with the same quote:

> I spent a long time trying to come to grips with my doubts, when suddenly I realized that I had better come to grips with what I believe. I have since moved from the agony of questions that I cannot answer to the reality of answers that I cannot escape . . . and it's a great relief!

This quote made a profound impact on my life, and I've since shared it with millions of men around the world. You see, I have struggled with doubt. I come from Missouri, the "Show Me State," and if I were in a tribe, it would be the Tribe of Doubting Thomas. I have questions about life, the Scriptures, and God that I still cannot answer. But as a man I realized I had to determine what I *do* know and what I *do* believe. Ordering my life around what I believe is ultimately what propelled me to step up and become a man.

What about you? Are you living your life based upon what you know to be true, or are you waffling because you haven't come to grips with your doubts and determined what you believe? Are you majoring in the minors (things that, in the end, do not matter), or are you majoring in the majors?

> ORDERING MY LIFE AROUND
> WHAT I BELIEVE IS ULTIMATELY
> WHAT PROPELLED ME TO
> STEP UP AND BECOME A MAN.

THE MOST IMPORTANT DECISION: STEPPING UP BY KNEELING DOWN

Your first step may be like the one I made before my junior year of college. Receiving Christ as my Savior and Lord demanded faith and courage like no other decision in my life, and it remains the most important commitment I've ever made.

Perhaps the most courageous thing you've ever done is before you right now in how you respond to the claims of Jesus Christ. I was afraid of what it would mean to give God my life and let Him be in control. Is there something you are afraid of? What is keeping you from the absolute surrender of your life to Christ? For me, I had a greater fear that I would miss God and, ultimately, the life He had designed for me.

If you haven't already surrendered your life to Christ, may I invite you to courageously kneel down and surrender to Him so that you can ultimately step up and be the man God made you to be? (If you are wondering what this looks like, I've included a piece titled "Knowing God Personally" in the back of this book to guide you.)

Of course, once you've made the decision to yield your life to Christ, the rest of your life lies ahead. There are some additional decisions that will mark your passage as a man.

> NO MAN WILL UNDERSTAND WHO
> HE IS AND WHAT HIS ULTIMATE
> ASSIGNMENT ON PLANET EARTH
> IS APART FROM KNOWING GOD.

The first is: Will you let God define your identity as a man? When a man defines himself and attempts to determine his identity apart from God, he is left to compare himself with others—a low and dangerous standard. A real man finds his essence and identity in his Creator.

No man will understand who he is and what his ultimate assignment on planet Earth is apart from knowing God. This is why A. W. Tozer said, "What comes into our minds when we think about God is the most important thing about us."[1]

In fact, I believe that one of the reasons we're short of real men today is that we've lost the fear of God. The majority of proverbs in the Old Testament were written by a father to his son to introduce him to God and equip him for life. Proverbs 1:7 tells us clearly, "The fear of the LORD is the beginning of knowledge; fools despise wisdom and instruction." The word *wisdom* is an important word for men. It means that we are to have skill in everyday living. We are to live life skillfully, the way our Creator designed it to be lived. Fearing God is the starting point for being a real man.

To fear God means that I hold Him in reverential awe. It means I see

Him for who He is—the sovereign King. When I revere God for who He is, I can rightly determine who I am as a man.

As I study Scripture and understand who God is, I realize that I am not the center of the universe. God is. I realize that I don't call the shots in life. God does.

This means I humble myself in submission to Him. I make choices realizing that God is everywhere present, sees all, and knows all. I live my life not to please myself but to please Him. I understand that I will someday give an account of my life to God and that His presence in my life motivates me to turn away from temptation, evil, and sin.

MY ROCK AND FOUNDATION

Another decision you must make moment by moment that will mark your life as a man is this: Will you center your life (your decisions, values, and priorities) on your relationship with God and the truth of God's Word?

I received a good lesson on this truth years ago when I went on a rock-climbing trip with several colleagues. Our supervisor thought this adventure would build leadership qualities and teamwork skills in all of us. I was hoping I could learn leadership some other way because I hate heights. But no such luck. I wound up in the Sierra Nevada Mountains among the rock-domed peaks, along with several sadists called "trainers," and eleven other guys foolish enough to be "trainees."

We spent the first day learning basic climbing techniques, and the next morning I was told we were going to rappel off the top of a cliff. I said, "Oh, really, where is it?"

They said, "Right up there."

We were standing on the floor of a valley, and I looked up fifteen hundred feet to a dome directly overhead. *How are we getting up there?* I wanted to know.

Well, the climb went better than I expected, and I loved the view from the top. But then I realized that getting down would be a bit more troublesome.

Rappelling is not that complicated. You back up to the edge of the cliff to the point where you can no longer stand on your feet; then you push off and let the rope hold you. Several times I inspected the area where the rope was securely fastened to bolts sunk into the rock. There were four of those bolts, and I wanted to know, What were the bolts made of? How far did they go into the rock? How long had they been there, and above all, would they hold me?

My trainers assured me they had never lost anyone before. Besides, some guys a lot bigger and heavier than I had rappelled off this precipice with no problem. In fact, one guy had gone off in a wheelchair.

All these words did little to slow down the vibration of my knocking knees, but finally I began backing off the cliff. When I came to the point where I was totally horizontal, I looked back over my shoulder (something you're not supposed to do), and everything came clearly into focus. At that point the phrase "do or die" never seemed more relevant. I decided I had to go for it and pushed off.

And the rope held.

Did I become an enthusiastic rock climber after this? No, I haven't done it since! But I did learn a lot about faith that day. I learned that you have to believe the rope will hold you. You have to lean against and trust yourself to the rope. And I learned that walking with God, and making Christ your Lord, is just like rappelling down a cliff. You lean back and push off with the knowledge that God is your rope. He is worthy of your trust every moment of every day.

These are the things *I believe.*

You see, I spent a long time trying to come to grips with my doubts, when suddenly I realized I had better come to grips with what I believe.

I have since moved from the "agony of questions that I cannot answer to the reality of answers that I cannot escape . . . and it's a great relief!"

It really has been a relief since I placed my trust in Jesus Christ in the summer of 1968. And it can be for you, too.

Want to think about *Stepping Up* a little more or discuss it with your friends? Visit FamilyLife.com/Resources for a list of questions and talking points.

THE FOURTH STEP:
MENTOR

An Age of Investment
and Impact

18

A MAJOR LEAGUE
TRAILBLAZER

*There is no power on earth that can neutralize
the influence of a high, simple and useful life.*

—BOOKER T. WASHINGTON

Jackie Robinson didn't see much of a future for himself in professional baseball.[1] The year was 1945, and he was twenty-six. A UCLA graduate and World War II veteran, he was trying to make a living by playing for the Kansas City Monarchs of the Negro American League. He hadn't played much baseball; he was better known as a football star at UCLA. But when the Monarchs offered him a job, he decided to give it a try.

Jackie was infuriated by the indignities that black ballplayers faced. In some stadiums, they weren't allowed to use the locker rooms because white owners didn't like the idea of black men using the showers. He hated the segregated hotels and drinking fountains. In one instance, when the team bus stopped for gas and the station owner said the players couldn't use his restroom, Robinson threatened to fill up the team's bus at another station. The owner changed his mind.

And, of course, the worst indignity of all was the fact that Major League Baseball was segregated. For decades, some of the best baseball players in the nation—legends like Satchel Paige and Josh Gibson—were kept out of the big leagues. Robinson saw no hope for the situation changing, or for the opportunity to move up and play baseball in the whites-only major leagues. "I began to wonder why I should dedicate my life to a career where the boundaries for progress were set by racial discrimination," he later wrote.[2]

A LEGENDARY MEETING

Robinson was contacted by Branch Rickey, general manager of the Brooklyn Dodgers. Word was that Rickey was forming a new Negro league and wanted to talk with Robinson about joining it.

Robinson's meeting with Rickey on August 28, 1945, became a turning point in America's history. Robinson learned that Rickey had no intention of starting another Negro league. Instead, he wanted to break the color barrier in professional baseball . . . and he wanted Jackie Robinson to lead the way by joining the Brooklyn Dodgers.

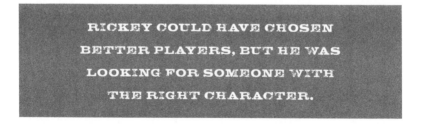

RICKEY COULD HAVE CHOSEN BETTER PLAYERS, BUT HE WAS LOOKING FOR SOMEONE WITH THE RIGHT CHARACTER.

Rickey could have chosen better players, but he was looking for someone with the right character. He had no illusions about the pressure that the first black ballplayer would face—the hatred he would encounter from white players and the impossible expectations he would feel from the black community. He wanted someone who was angry about segregation but could keep that anger in check. Choose the wrong player, he felt, and he would push the cause back by years.

"If you're a good enough man, we can make this a start in the right direction," Rickey told Robinson. "But let me tell you, it's going to take an awful lot of courage."

In the meeting, Rickey confronted Robinson with examples of the situations he would face. He acted the part of ballplayers using racial slurs and trying to start fights. "They'll taunt and goad you," he said. "They'll try to provoke a race riot in the ballpark. This is the way to prove to the public that a Negro should not be allowed in the major league."

"Mr. Rickey," Robinson said, "are you looking for a Negro who is afraid to fight back?"

"No," Rickey replied, "I'm looking for a ballplayer with guts enough not to fight back."

Robinson wondered if he was the right person for this. Did he have that kind of strength and courage? "Yet I knew that I must," Robinson later wrote. "I had to do it for so many reasons. For black youth, for my mother, for Rae [his wife], for myself."[3]

HANDLING THE PRESSURE

Rickey turned out to be an accurate prophet. After a successful year in the minor leagues, Robinson made his major-league debut as the Dodgers' first baseman in April of 1947. The first resentment he faced was from his own teammates. They didn't like the idea of a black player taking a white man's spot on the roster. Many were from the south and weren't accustomed to equal treatment for blacks.

Dixie Walker, one of the top Brooklyn players, worried about the reaction back home in Hueytown, Alabama, if he played with blacks. He feared how it would affect business at his hardware and sporting-goods store. "I grew up in the South, and in those days you grew up in a different manner," Walker said years later. "We thought that blacks didn't have ice water in their veins and so [they] couldn't take the pressure of playing big league baseball."[4]

On opening day, most of the players ignored Robinson. He arrived in the locker room to discover that he hadn't been assigned a locker; his uniform was hanging on a hook on the wall.

Robinson's first real test occurred in a three-game series with the Philadelphia Phillies. A flood of insults poured out of the Philadelphia dugout during the game. The Phillies insulted his appearance and yelled about the diseases he would pass on to the Dodger players and their wives.

Robinson took insults like these personally. "For one wild and rage-crazed minute," he wrote later, "I thought, 'To hell with Mr. Rickey's noble experiment.' I thought what a glorious, cleansing thing it would be to let go. To hell with the image of the patient black freak I was supposed to create. I would throw down my bat, stride over to the Phillies dugout, grab one of those white sons of bitches and smash his teeth in with my despised black fist. Then I could walk away from it all."[5]

But Robinson withstood the temptation that day . . . and for the entire season. Instead, he let his playing speak for him. It was more than his hitting and fielding, which improved throughout the season. He also disrupted the opposing team with his daring base running. He would take impossibly big leads off base, throwing pitchers out of their rhythm and shaking their confidence. This led to more walks and better pitches for his teammates to hit. He could take over a game even if he never got a hit.

Still, he paid a price for holding back his emotions. At home he became withdrawn from his wife, Rachel, and found it difficult to sleep. At one point he called his sister and said, "I can't take it anymore. I'm quitting."

He received almost no support from his teammates, who excluded him from social outings and hardly spoke to him on road trips. The players' wives met regularly for shopping, knitting, and impromptu sleepovers, but Rachel was never invited.

ROOTING FOR JACKIE ROBINSON

But as the season progressed, things began to change. His teammates began yelling in his defense at opposing teams, threatening retaliation if the insults continued. He was greeted by well-wishers and autograph seekers wherever he went. White kids began selling, "I'm rooting for Jackie Robinson" buttons at Ebbets Field.

Most of the letters the Dodgers received were encouraging. One fan wrote, "You've got a lot more friends in this country of ours than enemies. The main thing to remember is that it's the unthinking few who generally make the biggest noise." Another said, "If your batting average never gets any higher than .100 and if you make an error every inning, [and] if I can raise my boy to be half the man that you are, I'll be a happy father."[6]

Robinson also began to see the impact he was having on the culture. An owner of an electronics factory in New Jersey, for example, was inspired by Robinson's example and decided to integrate his factory.

Late in the season, Brooklyn fans were angered when Enos Slaughter of the St. Louis Cardinals appeared to deliberately step on Robinson's foot at first base. One fan, Doug Wilder, was at the game that day, and he felt this may have been Robinson's greatest moment "in showing how he would rise over and over to be the person he was. . . . It was a tremendous lesson."[7] Later in life, Wilder went into politics in Virginia and became the first African American in the United States to become a governor.

Robinson was named the National League's Rookie of the Year in 1947, and he helped lead the Dodgers to the World Series, where they lost to the

New York Yankees. After the final game of the series, each of his teammates came by his locker to congratulate him for the season.

He had succeeded in integrating the major leagues; in fact, by the end of the 1947 season, there were other black players in baseball. But his greatest impact may have been in the broader American culture. As Arnold Rampersad wrote in his biography of Robinson,

> Over a period of six months, from the first stumbling steps to the victories that closed the season, he had revolutionized the image of black Americans in the eyes of many whites. Starting out as a token, he had utterly complicated their sense of the nature of black people, how they thought and felt, their dignity and their courage in the face of adversity. No black American man had ever shone so brightly for so long as the epitome not only of stoic endurance but also of intelligence, bravery, physical power, and grit. Because baseball was lodged so deeply in the average white man's psyche, Robinson's protracted victory had left an intimate mark there.[8]

20/20 GENERATIONAL VISION

Jackie Robinson wasn't forced to become the man to integrate Major League Baseball. Branch Rickey could have found another player, and it certainly would have been more comfortable for Robinson to follow someone else's lead. He had the ability, however, to look beyond himself. Someone needed to make the sacrifice. Someone needed to blaze the trail so that others in the future would have equal opportunities.

I think that many of us men face a similar choice as we reach our thirties, forties, and fifties. We may never face the intense opposition that confronted Robinson, but I believe we are called to look beyond ourselves to the impact we can have on the next generation.

> WE MAY NEVER FACE THE INTENSE
> OPPOSITION THAT CONFRONTED
> ROBINSON, BUT I BELIEVE WE ARE
> CALLED TO LOOK BEYOND OURSELVES
> TO THE IMPACT WE CAN HAVE ON
> THE NEXT GENERATION.

Becoming a mentor is the fourth of the five steps of manhood. Some guys can see clearly where they are in life, but they haven't developed the ability, like Robinson did, to look past themselves. A mentor, on the other hand, exhibits "20/20 generational vision." He sees the need to pass on his faith and his experience to "faithful men who will be able to teach others also" (2 Timothy 2:2). A mentor makes decisions and orders his life to intentionally invest in the next generation.

A mentor must pass on his values; lessons learned from his mistakes, successes, and defeats; the essence of his life. He intentionally passes on wisdom to the next generation and casts a vision for how they can do the same.

It's possible to step up and become a mentor when you are a young man, especially if you are put in a position of authority or influence over others. But in this section, I'm going to speak primarily to those of you who are entering what I call the "prime time" years.

Most younger men pour their physical and emotional energy into building their careers, raising their families, and being involved in church or community. Once their children leave home, I've often seen men head in one of three directions:

1. They pour their energy into a renewed effort to capitalize on their position and experience and seek further success and influence in the working world.

2. Perhaps fearing the onset of older age, they regress and try to recapture their youth by seeking adventure and sensual pleasure.

3. Realizing that they won't achieve the wealth and success they had dreamed about in their careers, they gradually become depressed and passive and end up squandering the assets God has given them.

But there is a better path—a path of wisdom. Many men in the prime-time years recognize that they now have the time and energy to broaden their influence and impact for Christ by mentoring younger men.

If you are at this stage in life, my challenge to you is to step up and become a mentor. You'll find the "view" from this step to be quite exhilarating.

Want to think about *Stepping Up* a little more or discuss it with your friends? Visit FamilyLife.com/Resources for a list of questions and talking points.

19

MEN NEED
OTHER MEN

*Some men sailed with the wind until that
decisive moment in history when events
propelled them into the center of the storm.*

—JOHN F. KENNEDY, *Profiles in Courage*

Question: Besides your father, what men have had the most influence in making you the man you are today?

Many of us can reflect on the influence of a boss, a friend, a teacher, or an older man who had a simple belief in us. Several men would list an athletic coach from their youth—there's something about the training and admonition of a coach, combined with the ups and downs of athletic competition, that etches lasting memories into the minds of young men.

Our paths cross with many people during our lifetimes, but only a few have a significant impact in our lives. Most often, these are the ones who take a personal interest in passing on their knowledge, wisdom, and experience. They are mentors.

When I think of those who have mentored me over the years, my mind focuses on men like these:

- Don Meredith (a fellow Campus Crusade staff member), who helped ignite a vision in me for marriage and family.
- H. D. McCarty, my college pastor, who listened to my wild ideas and gently guided me into a love for Jesus Christ.
- Bill Bright, who modeled wise leadership for the thirty-three years I worked for him, believed in me, and asked my opinion on important matters.
- Dr. Howard Hendricks, who believed in me and has repeatedly gave me his time and his wisdom.
- Steve Robinson, a friend who realized that coaching me in my golf game was hopeless, but who did coach me in the discipline of marketing.
- Crawford Loritts, a buddy who didn't know how to catch a fish until I taught him . . . and a valued counselor in helping me be more effective cross-culturally.
- Ed Ligon, who saved my bacon in the eighties, when FamilyLife was growing 40 percent a year, and mentored me as a leader.
- Merle Engle, a real friend, who modeled servant-leadership in innumerable ways.
- Bob Lepine, a mentor in radio who, in the process, became a trustworthy friend.
- Scott Beck, who came alongside me as a mentor at pivotal times and, in the process, became an authentic friend.

Many others have taught me about life, about faith, and about relationships. Looking back on it all, I should be smarter, better balanced, and more effective than I am! But because of the investments these men have made in me, I am truly blessed! As one man said, "Dennis, some men can live a lifetime and have only one man who has stood alongside them, but you have several. You are a wealthy man."

I agree.

As I think about these experiences, I'm reminded of what a mentor once told me: "The greatest impact of a man's life is between the ages of fifty and seventy-five."

Men, did you hear that? Your life isn't over when you get your first AARP invitation.

It could be just beginning.

EVERY MAN NEEDS A MENTOR

A mentor is a life coach—a tutor and instructor who recognizes that he has the privilege and duty of passing a baton in a generational relay race. Stepping up and becoming a mentor can be one of the most definitive and courageous steps a man makes in his lifetime.

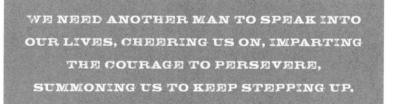

WE NEED ANOTHER MAN TO SPEAK INTO OUR LIVES, CHEERING US ON, IMPARTING THE COURAGE TO PERSEVERE, SUMMONING US TO KEEP STEPPING UP.

Every man *needs* a mentor, and every man needs to *be* a mentor. We need another man to speak into our lives, cheering us on, imparting the courage to persevere, summoning us to keep stepping up. In turn, we need to mentor others. This is our generational responsibility.

Understand this, however: to ask a man to mentor you takes courage, and to become a mentor takes even more.

The greatest proof that mentoring requires courage is that so few men do it.

OBSTACLES TO MENTORING

When it comes to being a mentor, many men suffer from self-doubt. They question whether they have anything of value to share with a younger man. Or they worry that they don't know how. Men reason that they aren't qualified or have no training. Mentoring can be viewed as an assignment only for those who have a certain personality or gifting. One man posted this statement on my Facebook page when I mentioned that I was writing about mentoring: "I seriously doubt that I would ever be a mentor, as I'm not one of the 'visible' or 'popular' men in my church."

> **A MAN'S LEGACY INVOLVES BELIEVING IN AND EMPOWERING YOUNGER MEN.**

Some see mentoring as something they do only in the workplace. Others are unwilling to set aside their desires for how they will spend their time. A few want to mentor younger men but don't know where to find someone.

To become a mentor requires the courage to press through these obstacles, acknowledging that life is about more than your agenda, or your pleasure. It means ignoring your feelings of inadequacy or fears of failure and getting involved in the lives of younger men who need to be challenged to step up. A man's legacy involves believing in and empowering younger men.

I recall wondering if I had anything to offer younger men, so I decided to compile a list of life lessons. As I unearthed my "inventory," I found that many of my best lessons weren't from my successes but from my failures, mistakes, and poor decisions. Through these I've learned the great value of perseverance—a lesson that I find myself passing on to many men who are straining under the weight of their own blunders. "Courage doesn't always roar," writes Mary Anne Radmacher. "Sometimes courage is the quiet voice at the end of the day saying, 'I will try again tomorrow.'"[1]

THE REWARD

When Michael asked me to mentor him, I was honored and afraid. I had absolutely no idea how to be a mentor or what the process entailed. It was like standing on the edge of a cliff, forty feet above a river, full of fears and uncertainty but realizing I needed to jump. So I leaped up and out into what felt like thin air.

We'd meet over lunch once a month and chat about challenges he was facing and lessons I was learning. This man-to-man encouragement went on for several months until finally Michael felt safe enough to confess the issue that was sucking the life out of his marriage and family: debt. A new pickup truck on payments, a nice new home with a fat mortgage, and more than thirty thousand dollars of credit-card debt.

When Michael dumped all that red ink on the table where we were having lunch, he knew it was time to clean up his act. He knew I loved him. And he knew that the jig was up. It was "D-day"—deliverance from debt.

I challenged him: "Melt your credit cards." Which he did.

"Sell your truck." Which he did.

"Downsize your house." Which he did.

"Begin paying off all these debts." Which he has done.

That was nearly a decade ago, and as I am writing these words, I think about an e-mail that Michael recently sent me: "I'm eternally grateful for the investment you made in me. You encouraged me to 'be the man' on my fortieth birthday, and you gave me the definition of 'being the man.'"

Guys, this is the reward that God designed every man to experience.

THROWING DOWN THE GAUNTLET

As a man stands on the manhood step, it's a good thing to be facing upward, thinking about mentoring. As you contemplate becoming a mentor, I want to encourage you to begin asking God to give you a couple of men to mentor. This may not be the most courageous thing you've ever done, but I promise you, it will be one of the most important and satisfying things you will ever do as a man.

THE VALUE OF FINDING A MENTOR

Here are just a few of the things I've learned from mentors who've come alongside me through the years:

- The best measure of what a man can do is what a man has done.
- Making bad decisions helps you learn to make good decisions.
- Once the facts are clear, usually the right decision jumps out at you.
- Communication is not what is said but what is heard.
- Every man needs margin in his calendar for the unexpected at work and at home.
- No amount of success at work will compensate for failure at home.
- Debt is dangerous.
- Lifelong male friendships are challenging, but every man needs a friend who can speak truth into his life.

- A man needs to be accountable to another man.
- Praying with his wife is the most powerful thing a husband can do every day.
- Every man is leaving a legacy, so why not be intentional about the legacy you leave?
- A life lived without God, the Scriptures, and complete, daily surrender to Jesus Christ is a wasted life.

Want to think about *Stepping Up* a little more or discuss it with your friends? Visit FamilyLife.com/Resources for a list of questions and talking points.

20

BECOMING A
GENERATIONAL
MESSENGER

It is the righteous man who lives
for the next generation.

—DIETRICH BONHOEFFER

My friend Crawford Loritts has a vision for building into the lives of younger men who are leaders. In 2003 Crawford invited me and nine other men to join forty younger men in a two-day conference on mentoring. At the end of the event, all ten of us older men had four younger men that we agreed to mentor, one-on-one, for the next twelve months. We all signed a written agreement and began to meet—either in person or over the phone—on a monthly basis.

Nearly a decade later, I am still meeting with two of those men, who are now in their thirties. We talk about loving our wives and children, about schedules, priorities, pace, and just about every gritty issue a man faces. It's confidential. It's safe. And I think it's encouraging to these younger men.

We've been fishing and duck hunting together. They talk and I listen. They ask, and I try to answer. Sometimes I ask them questions. On other occasions I speak into their lives. We've read and discussed books and Scripture.

Spending time with these young men and building a friendship with them has been one of the greatest privileges of my life. The experience has resulted in a conviction that life is about how we can serve and equip the next generation.

OUTLIVING OURSELVES

God designed men to be "generational messengers"—sending messages of character, values, and vision through other men to a time beyond our horizon. We were made to outlive ourselves, generationally speaking, by mentoring younger men.

This pattern is modeled in the apostle Paul's relationship with a young man named Timothy. Near the end of Paul's life, he challenged Timothy with a compelling vision for being a viral spiritual multiplier, a mentor:

> You therefore, my son, be strong in the grace that is in Christ Jesus. The things which you have heard from me in the presence of many witnesses, entrust these to faithful men who will be able to teach others also. (2 Timothy 2:1–2)

Note that Paul spoke of influencing multiple generations: he mentored Timothy, who passed on what he learned to "faithful men" who would then "teach others also"—a relay race of at least four generations.

We don't know what happened to Timothy's father, but we do know that Timothy needed an older man in his life. Mentors are, in many ways, father figures to the young men they train. In fact, I am seeing this kind of relationship beautifully played out in the life of my friend Bill.

Bill has a teenage son, and his son has a friend whose father died nearly two years ago. Bill is a great dad and is quite involved in his son's life. And he now includes this other young man, his son's friend, in many of their father-son activities. The three of them do guy stuff together, and once a week they go to breakfast, where they read through Proverbs and talk about what they're learning.

I love what Bill—and his son—are doing for this young man. And you might be interested to know that Bill is simply passing on some of what he received when he was a young man. "I had a family who reached out to me when I was fatherless," Bill explains. "Mr. Reed took me and his son Mike (my best friend) fishing and on trips. I was at their house more than at mine. He even paid for a bike my mother gave me (I found out later that he paid for it). This past summer, the Reeds celebrated their fiftieth [wedding] anniversary with a party of family and friends. I had the privilege of being introduced as their second son."

In a culture where 40 percent of children are being born to a single-parent mom, do *not* underestimate the power of an older man in a young man's life!

There's something in the chest of every man that draws him to be a mentor. It's the DNA of true manhood, and these genetics run throughout Scripture—young men seeking out the gray-haired men and valuing their wisdom. Elders commissioned to spread life lessons on to the next generation.

In whatever way you choose to follow this biblical pattern, there are three qualities that describe how a mentor can maximize his influence.

1. A Mentor Is Available

A number of years ago, I was making a presentation over lunch to Don Soderquist, former chief operating officer (COO) of Walmart. I was briskly moving through my charts and graphs to arrive at the part I was most excited about—the slide showing how FamilyLife had grown more than 600 percent in ten years.

All of a sudden it struck me who I was talking to, and I began to chuckle.

Surprised, Don asked, "Why are you laughing?"

I smiled and replied, "It just hit me that I'm talking to *you* about the 'huge growth' of this little nonprofit organization."

As COO he had overseen growth from zero to two hundred billion dollars!

Don laughed with me and listened as I finished the presentation. He was very gracious as he shared some stories about his leadership journey and experiences. In our conversation he happened to mention that one of his strengths was leading with vision.

WHAT IMPRESSED ME MOST
WAS THAT HE GAVE ME HIS TIME.

The meeting went so well that at the end of my presentation, I asked if he would spend a day with me, mentoring me on the things he'd learned about vision. He said yes. Six months later I drove back to his office in northwest Arkansas with a couple dozen questions and a recorder. The lessons and wisdom he shared were priceless.

But it wasn't just what he said that was important. What impressed me most was that he gave me his time.

You are likely very busy. But being available to a young man who wants to be mentored may be one of the most strategic investments you'll ever make. You may be used by God to save a man's job, his marriage, his family, or even his life.

2. A Mentor Is Purposeful

As a mentor, you are taking a young man to a place he wouldn't go by himself. A mentor knows what a younger man needs and sharpens him by speaking the truth to him.

Recently I began mentoring Jim and asked him to tell me his life story. His ninety-minute synopsis was filled with painful stories of how his father had abandoned him, how he'd been abused by an older man as a teenager, and the impact of these circumstances on his life as a husband and father. At the end of our conversation, I told Jim that I was going to be sending him a book that I had written, and I wanted him to begin reading it at his own pace. I purposely didn't tell him anything about the book.

When Jim opened the package a week later and found my book, *The Best Gift You Can Ever Give Your Parents*, he cursed. But he started reading, and he is processing what it means to honor his father. Although this is a new mentoring relationship for me, I am confident that Jim is about to embrace the "Forgotten Commandment": "Honor your father and your mother" (Exodus 20:12). I also believe that he will one day be able to write a tribute to his dad and read it to him.

A mentor purposefully builds life lessons into those he mentors. As you consider being a mentor, think through what makes life work for you—at work, at home, and in your relationship with Christ. What have you learned about the following?

- handling pressure and balancing the pace of life
- working with people
- building and keeping friendships with other men
- investing in your marriage
- resolving conflict
- facing unexpected crises or tragedy

- managing your finances
- developing a real relationship with God
- reading, understanding, and applying the Scriptures
- raising your children
- developing the type of character needed to succeed at work
- growing through failure

And don't forget to ask yourself, What's the most courageous thing I've ever done in my life?

In thinking about these issues, you'll likely realize that you may have more to share than you thought.

3. A Mentor Is Authentic

Effective mentors are gritty and real. On this step there is no room for pretenders, egomaniacs, or wimps. Only real men stand here.

A number of years ago, I spent a day getting advice from a man who had far more leadership experience than I had. One of the questions I asked him was about his darkest days as a leader. What were they, and how did he handle them?

What I heard were two stories of betrayal and disappointment. I appreciated his transparency as he described moments of discouragement, doubt, and even despair. He didn't airbrush his story. He painted the picture realistically, blemishes and all.

In the years that have followed, I've faced a few of those moments myself. Because this leader was willing to be authentic, I've reflected often on how he handled a rough situation, and I've pressed on. And I've passed on some of what I've learned in those valleys to the men I mentor.

A mentor's willingness to strip away the veneer and allow a younger man to smell the stench of raw humanity when things didn't work out may be the greatest life lesson he has to share.

Some of you who read these words will decide to courageously step up and ask God to guide you to a young man to mentor. You may find such a person in your place of work, in your church, in your neighborhood or community, or around a hobby or sport you share with other men. It could be a mentoring relationship established over the Internet through a safe and secure online service, such as FamilyLife's eMentoring program. (Visit FamilyLife.com to learn more about this resource.) It could mean that you could join your wife in mentoring a young couple as they begin their marriage. Or you may start hosting a small-group study, such as the Home-Builders Couples Series®, with several younger couples.

Selecting a person to mentor may be as simple as saying yes to a request, or it may likely mean that as a man you develop a spiritual receptivity to those God brings your way. As I look to the future, I expect and pray that I'll have four to six men I'll be mentoring for the rest of my life.

A DIVINE ASSIGNMENT

I live in the country, and for a number of years I've jogged on roads near my home for exercise. I'm embarrassed to say that I jogged by Lee, and the shack he lived in, for a decade before I began to sense that I should offer to help him.

One day I introduced myself to Lee, who was twenty-nine years old and was paralyzed from the waist down, the result of a childhood asthma attack and an adverse reaction to a drug. His father deserted him, and when Lee was ten, his mom declared, "You are damaged goods."

For years Lee and his mom barely scraped by, living off welfare checks until his cousin helped Lee buy a riding lawn mower. That became Lee's only mode of transportation, and his only ability to make additional money by mowing nearby lawns.

It became very clear that Lee had a lot more courage than most men. He could easily have been a victim and given up. I discovered that Lee had graduated from high school with a GPA (grade point average) of 3.3, and that shortly after his mom's death, he had placed his faith in Christ as his Savior and Lord. I also discovered that he tithed from his monthly welfare and disability checks from the State, which combined were a mere $550. With his mom's recent death, things were very tight. He wondered how he would survive.

> AS I LOOK TO THE FUTURE, I EXPECT
> AND PRAY THAT I'LL HAVE FOUR
> TO SIX MEN I'LL BE MENTORING
> FOR THE REST OF MY LIFE.

Lee had never been employed. I asked if he wanted a job, and I'll never forget his response: "You know, I'd like someone else to get that welfare money, someone who really needs it." So I set Lee up with an old computer and a typing manual and told him to call me when he was typing forty words per minute. He did, and then he came to work for FamilyLife.

There's so much more to Lee's story—how he learned to drive, how he learned to buy (and then wreck) a truck, how he began going to college, how he tore down the shack and replaced it with a nice mobile home. He met the governor of Arkansas, who then introduced him to the president of the United States.

Lee needed a man to believe in him. A man who'd mentor him. In my professional career, I've had many privileges, but watching Lee take some of the most courageous steps I've ever seen a man take remains one of the greatest privileges of my life.

We all want to be remembered—to leave a legacy, to make a difference. If your family is nearly grown, and you are on the manhood step looking upward, then you are in your prime-time years. I believe your best years are ahead. You may be asking, How can I best leverage the experience, gifts, and talents in the next season of my life? Well, I have something I'd like you to consider: Why don't you ask God to give you 20/20 generational vision, and invest your life in the next generation of men?

As a mentor, you can make a difference in another man's life that can change his whole world. As someone once said, "To the world, you may just be somebody. But to somebody, you may just be the world."

Want to think about *Stepping Up* a little more or discuss it with your friends? Visit FamilyLife.com/Resources for a list of questions and talking points.

THE FIFTH STEP:
PATRIARCH

An Age of Influence
and Relevance

21

LEFT BEHIND

*Mountaineering tends to draw men and women not easily deflected
from their goals. . . . Unfortunately, the sort of individual who is
programmed to ignore personal distress and keep pushing for the top
is frequently programmed to disregard signs of grave and imminent
danger as well. This forms the nub of a dilemma that every Everest
climber eventually comes up against: in order to succeed you must be
exceedingly driven, but if you're too driven you're likely to die. . . .
Thus the slopes of Everest are littered with corpses.*

—JON KRAKAUER, *Into Thin Air*

When Beck Weathers opened his eyes, he thought he was safe and warm in
his bed at home. But then, after he looked at his right hand—a "grey and
lifeless thing"—and realized it was frozen solid, he knew this wasn't Texas.[1]

He was lying alone in the snow, in a howling wind at 26,000 feet on
Mount Everest. He realized he had been left behind by his fellow climbers—
they must have thought he was dead.

He thought of his wife and two children. They were so clear in his mind,
as if he could touch them. And he had what he calls an epiphany. "I knew at

that instant, with absolute clarity, that if I did not stand at once, I would spend an eternity on that spot."[2]

He wasn't ready to die.

A PERFECT DAY FOR CLIMBING

Weathers, a pathologist and an enthusiastic mountaineer, was part of a group of fifteen climbers who had set out a day earlier to reach the top of Mount Everest. They started out in the middle of the morning, the first of three groups attempting the summit that day, May 10, 1996. The temperature was well below zero, and the stars shined so brightly that the climbers could see their reflections in the ice. A perfect day for climbing.

On mountains like Everest, the descent is often more dangerous than the climb. Their goal was to reach the summit by 2:00 p.m., at the latest, allowing them enough time, energy, and bottled oxygen to return to their camp by dark. Just the year before, group leader Rob Hall had decided to turn his clients around before the summit when he saw they didn't have enough time to ensure a safe descent.

Weathers had trained well for this adventure and was in fine physical condition, but he ran into an unexpected problem: his eyesight began to fail. It was a high-altitude side effect from eye surgery he'd undergone eighteen months before to improve his sight.

He thought things would improve with daylight, but they didn't. At 7:30 a.m., Hall told him he couldn't continue if his vision didn't improve. And it was too dangerous to descend by himself to the camp. Hall made Weathers promise to wait at that spot until he returned in a few hours.

That was the last he saw of Hall.

At noon, three members of the group came by, reporting that they had turned back because the three climbing groups had caused such a traffic jam, they realized they wouldn't reach the summit in time. They urged

Weathers to go down with them, but he had committed to Hall and felt he needed to stay.

"I WAS BEGINNING TO LOSE IT"

Weathers later learned that Hall had unwisely allowed several in the group to continue on to the summit, despite the delays. Hall and one client didn't leave the summit until nearly 4:00 p.m. Meanwhile, Weathers was down below, still waiting, barely able to see.

More members of his group returned and reported that Hall was hours behind. So after waiting for more than ten hours, Weathers joined them on the descent. Because he couldn't see, he was "short-roped"—another climber tied a rope around Weathers's waist and then around his own, and then stayed above Beck on the descent. Several times Weathers took a step into thin air, and the rope saved him.

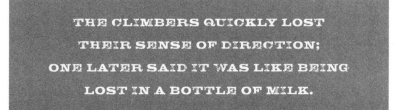

THE CLIMBERS QUICKLY LOST THEIR SENSE OF DIRECTION; ONE LATER SAID IT WAS LIKE BEING LOST IN A BOTTLE OF MILK.

And then an unexpected blizzard hit, complete with thunder, driving snow, and winds up to seventy miles per hour. The climbers quickly lost their sense of direction; one later said it was like being lost in a bottle of milk.

Weathers's right hand began getting cold, so he took off his first two layers of gloves to warm the hand against his chest. But it was so cold that the skin on his hand and arm instantly froze. Then he lost the gloves to the wind.

By midnight, the climbers were still lost. Then the weather cleared enough for them to briefly get their bearings and determine that the camp was a few hundred yards away. Weathers and three others were totally spent, and they realized their lives depended on someone getting back to the camp and sending help. They stayed behind, along with a healthier climber who looked after them.

"Sleep was our deadliest enemy," Weathers wrote later. "Every mountaineer knows that if you allow yourself to be taken down by that cold, it is a one-way ticket to death. There are no exceptions. Your core temperature plunges until your heart stops. So we yelled at each other, and hit each other and kicked each other. Anything to remain awake."[3]

Despite these efforts, Weathers and another climber, Yasuko Namba, began to drift into a comatose state as the storm continued to howl through the night. Their condition deteriorated to the point that when the others were finally rescued, they were left behind. As one climber said, "By then I assumed Yasuko was dead and Beck was a lost cause."[4]

The exhausted survivors back at camp actually had a much larger problem—many more climbers besides Yasuko and Beck were missing. The storm had trapped an unprecedented number of climbers on the mountain.

"AS CLOSE TO DEATH AS A PERSON CAN BE"

When the sun rose again, rescuers set out to find the missing. One group came across Namba and Weathers where they had been left behind on the trail. "Both bodies were partially buried," one of them said later. "Their faces and torsos were covered with snow; only their hands and feet were sticking out. The wind was just screaming."[5]

They were stunned to discover that Weathers and Namba were still alive. But Weathers, one of the rescuers said, "was as close to death as a person can be and still be breathing."[6]

Once again, they decided to leave Namba and Weathers behind because they were so close to death. In an emergency situation like this, with other climbers to rescue, it was important for the rescuers to conserve their energy for those who had the best chance to survive.

Weathers remained exposed to the elements for several more hours. And then, in his words, a miracle occurred. "I opened my eyes."[7]

"YOU CANNOT SWEAT THAT SMALL STUFF"

Once he realized where he was and determined that he was not ready to die, he forced himself to stand and begin heading toward camp. "Both my hands were completely frozen. My face was destroyed by the cold. I was profoundly hypothermic. I had not eaten in three days, or taken water for two days. I was lost and I was almost completely blind. *You cannot sweat that small stuff,* I said to myself. *You have to focus on that which must be done, and do that thing.*"[8]

He kept on falling and getting back up. He knew he needed to reach the camp by sundown, or he was doomed. Yet, to his surprise, that prospect didn't frighten him.

> I am not a particularly brave individual, and I would have expected myself to be terrified as I came to grips with that moment. But that was not what I felt at all.
>
> No, I was overwhelmed by an enormous, encompassing sense of melancholy. That I would never again say "I love you" to my wife, that I would never again hold my children, was just not acceptable.[9]

At 4:30 p.m., Weathers finally reached the camp. The other climbers were shocked to see him risen from the dead. "I couldn't believe what I saw," one said later. "This man had no face. It was completely black, solid black, like he had a crust over him. His jacket was unzipped down to his waist, full of snow. His right arm was bare and frozen over his head. We could not lower it. His skin looked like marble. White stone. No blood in it."[10]

"ANYBODY OUT THERE?"

Weathers was put in a tent, wrapped inside two sleeping bags with several hot-water bottles, and given an oxygen mask (remember, all this was still occurring at an elevation of 26,000 feet). His fellow climbers were convinced he wouldn't last another night.

TO EVERYONE'S AMAZEMENT, HE WAS STILL ALIVE.

Indeed, as darkness fell, a worse storm ripped across the mountain. The winds flattened the tent and ripped both sleeping bags away. Once again he was exposed to the wind and subzero temperatures for an entire night.

When Weathers heard other climbers packing up to leave the camp the next morning, he called out, "Hello! Anybody out there?"[11] To everyone's amazement, he was still alive.

He received medical treatment and responded so well that, with help, he was able to walk most of the way to the next two camps farther down the mountain. At one point he said, "They told me this trip was going to cost an arm and a leg. So far, I've gotten a little better deal."[12] Eventually he was airlifted out by helicopter.

The survival of Beck Weathers was one of the few happy endings on the deadliest day in the history of Mount Everest. Eight climbers perished, including group leader Rob Hall and Yasuko Namba, who had been left behind with Weathers but never woke from her coma.

Severe frostbite took its toll on Weathers, who had his right arm amputated below the elbow and lost all the fingers on his left hand. His nose was also amputated and reconstructed.

Today Weathers continues his practice as a doctor, but he is also an inspirational speaker. He tells audiences about his years of looking for meaning by climbing mountains, and his epiphany when he rose from the dead high on Mount Everest. "I searched all over the world for that which would fulfill me, and all along it was in my own backyard."[13]

His experience is one of my favorite tales of courage. And I also think it is a powerful metaphor for men as they enter into the last laps of life.

As I've met with men across the country, I've found that once they reach their sixties and seventies, they begin to feel just as "left behind" as Beck Weathers. Many begin to feel useless, as if their families, their churches, and their communities no longer need them. Some lose their vision, become passive, and stop acting like men. They think their years of impact and accomplishment are over.

Yet the Scriptures paint a different picture of this stage of life—it is a time when a man can perhaps have his greatest influence. But he must be willing to courageously step up if he doesn't want to be left behind.

Want to think about *Stepping Up* a little more or discuss it with your friends? Visit FamilyLife.com/Resources for a list of questions and talking points.

22

ARE YOU DONE MAKING A DIFFERENCE?

When your memories are more exciting
than your dreams, you've begun to die.

—HOWARD HENDRICKS

Stepping up and becoming a patriarch may be the most courageous step a man ever makes. It's not only politically incorrect, which makes an even stronger case for it, but it's countercultural, demanding grit and character to go against the grain of a youth-oriented society.

A man who doesn't step up at this point in his life will most assuredly step down. True patriarchs are such an endangered species that most men don't know this step exists. Others wrongly assume that they could never stand on this step; they don't see themselves ever becoming a patriarch. As a result, we have a generation of men entering this last season of their lives feeling aimless, useless, and bewildered, instead of being on the cutting edge of what could be their most productive and fruitful years.

About a dozen gray-haired men sat at the table in a prestigious country club, all former executives who had been highly successful. Leaders. Champions. Bright, intelligent minds. These were risk takers who'd led big lives, checkered with success and failure. Married between forty-five and sixty years, these men clearly had plenty to impart to younger generations. As I prepared to speak to them, I couldn't help but think that their gray heads only added to their dignity.

They had asked me to speak for ten minutes about what FamilyLife was doing to strengthen marriages and families. As I unpacked what we were doing, I mentioned that I would be speaking to a gathering of executives a couple of days later about "Three Qualities of a Patriarch."

What happened next was fascinating. It was as though I'd touched an open nerve. For forty-five minutes, they peppered me with questions, peeling back their hearts and sharing disappointments, frustrations, doubts, and desires.

They talked about how their adult children were critical of them, pushing them to the fringes of their lives. They were treated as unnecessary— except as babysitters—and they felt their family really didn't want their influence or their involvement. They said the only opportunities their churches offered were ushering, serving on the stewardship committee, and giving to building programs. They lamented that the culture had become so youth oriented, they felt emasculated—treated as though they were done and had nothing to give back.

These men—who had once been kings in their families, their businesses, and their communities—were for the first time in their lives uncertain what their roles should be. Like broken antiques gathering dust in the attic, they were without purpose.

But as they interacted, I could see in their eyes that they longed to be challenged again. War hardened and savvy, these sage soldiers wanted to fill their nostrils with the smoke of the battlefield and engage in the fight again. They really didn't want to trade their swords and armor for a five iron and a golf shirt. They realized they were made for something far nobler than watching cable news in a La-Z-Boy recliner.

> THESE MEN—WHO HAD ONCE BEEN KINGS IN THEIR FAMILIES, THEIR BUSINESSES, AND THEIR COMMUNITIES—WERE FOR THE FIRST TIME IN THEIR LIVES UNCERTAIN WHAT THEIR ROLES SHOULD BE.

I sat there astonished at what amounted to "grand theft"—men robbed of their glory—no longer dreaming because of a complicity of forces that had cruelly swindled them out of their courage to step up. Like Beck Weathers, these men had been left behind. Disoriented. Lost.

And like Weathers, if they didn't act soon, this last season of their lives would be wasted.

WHY ARE YOU HERE?

I left that meeting with two conclusions: First, most men don't know how to think about aging. They don't know what the Bible has to say about aging. Instead of facing upward on the fifth step and pursuing God and his purposes for their lives, they step down and squander a lifetime of experience, wisdom, and abilities. They erroneously conclude that their impact is over and take their cues from the culture about retirement. As they shrivel in self-absorption, all wrapped up in themselves, their lives become the smallest of packages. The result? A perennial shortage of sages.

Think with me for a moment: How many men do you know in their sixties, seventies, and eighties who are vigorous, still growing, and still using their influence for good? Men so visionary, so alive, so positive and expectant about how God is going to use them that you'd want to be like them when you grow old.

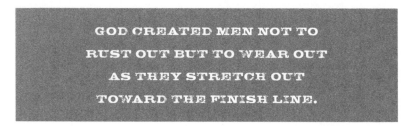

GOD CREATED MEN NOT TO
RUST OUT BUT TO WEAR OUT
AS THEY STRETCH OUT
TOWARD THE FINISH LINE.

A second conclusion was evident: It's time to resurrect the mantle of patriarch. It's time for a new order of noble, life-seasoned men to courageously arise, strip away encumbrances, and do battle on behalf of their children, grandchildren, communities, and nation. God created men not to rust out but to wear out as they stretch out toward the finish line.

For those of you who are over fifty-five years old—and especially if you are retired—I have a tough question: If you're finished making a difference, then why are you here?

Do you think your best days are behind you? Do you think you don't have anything else to give? Are you going to believe the culture that thinks you should clip coupons, collect seashells, and spend your kids' inheritance?

Or on the other hand, wouldn't you love to be able to articulate your mission for the years you have left? Wouldn't you like to know and feel noble about what you're living for?

Could you imagine others considering you to be . . . a patriarch?

PATRIARCH: A WORD THAT DRIPS
WITH DIGNITY

The word *patriarch* comes from the Latin word *patri*, which means "father." *Webster's* defines *patriarch* as it relates to a family as "a man who is a father or founder; the oldest representative of a group; a venerable [esteemed] old man."

Lest your imagination run away with you, I'm not suggesting that you become the Godfather, like Marlon Brando in the classic movie. Because of characters like him, unfortunately many consider *patriarch* a dirty word. For some it conjures images of male chauvinism, of dictatorial, self-serving men who rule their homes through fear, force, and manipulation.

Instead, *patriarch* is a word that glistens with prestige and nobility. In the Old Testament, patriarchs like Abraham, Isaac, and David served as heads of their families, and David was even described as a man after God's own heart (see 1 Samuel 13:14). Today, patriarchs are men who reach down the steps, investing in the generations to come. They are men who realize their potential to have a lasting influence in their families and communities.

Being a patriarch of your family isn't everything; it's not absolute authority, not domineering power, not manipulative control. But being the father of your family in your later years isn't nothing either! A patriarch understands his assignment, as well as where his influence lies, and he asks God to use him.

MY PERSONAL QUEST

I became interested in the concept of being a patriarch as my children grew into adults and began to marry. My role as a father was changing, and I knew that as they established their own families, I would no longer have the same authority in their lives. But I also recognized that my work as a father wasn't finished; it was just morphing in its expression. Even though my children were adults, they still needed my encouragement and prayers. I'm no longer the head coach calling the plays, but I've become a "fan" on the sidelines, cheering them on. Young men raising a family in this culture need a few raving fans, enthusiastic applause, and even an occasional standing ovation.

Finally, as patriarchs we have the time to cheer for our grandchildren and pass on stories of how God has worked in our lives. My nine-year-old grandson, James, asked me recently how I helped start FamilyLife. I gave him the *Reader's Digest* version of the story (perhaps I'll double back and tell him a little more in the coming days), which reminded me of Psalm 71, a psalm you might call the memoirs of a patriarch. In his old age, the psalmist declared,

O God, You have taught me from my youth,
And I still declare Your wondrous deeds.
And even when I am old and gray, O God, do not forsake me,
Until I declare Your strength to this generation,
Your power to all who are to come. (verses 17–18)

The generation to come needs to hear your stories of how you came to faith in Christ, how He answered your prayers, and how He provided for you and your family.

A NEW TITLE

What an opportunity we have as we enter into the final years of life to use the wisdom and influence we've accumulated and reach out to the next generation. This is the vision many men today need for their final years. I think of Bill Barber, a lifelong Texan with a wonderful, earthy sense of humor. I met Bill after his son Clay came to work at FamilyLife, and I called him a patriarch. He later wrote me to say he was surprised at my remark. "Heck, I didn't realize that I was one."

Bill said he's been called repulsive, obnoxious, anachronistic, funny, crazy, opinionated, a rascal, and "an enigma with savoir faire." But he kind of liked this new title of "patriarch."

"Fact is, I'm really loving this patriarching," he said. "It's a lot simpler than most of my peers think. You gotta quit fighting it. Admit your age. Oh, yes, it doesn't hurt to (1) be an encourager, (2) be a servant, (3) disciple, (4) sometimes be silent, and (5) be forgiving to others and yourself. Being a patriarch is just not too bad."

And it doesn't hurt that Bill, the patriarch, always has a pocketful of peppermint candy he hands out.

THEIR FINEST HOUR

I've found that men of all ages resonate with the call to become a patriarch. They *really* listen. They *want* dignity at the end of their lives. Intuitively, they *know* they were made for this—a profoundly mystical and powerful word that causes their chests to swell again. A uniquely masculine mantle. They realize that God still wants to use them, that their finest hours may still lie ahead.

The following poem by the Bishop of Exeter reminds us of our need for real men of all ages, but every time I read it, I think it best describes a patriarch:

Give Us Men!

Give us Men!
Men—from every rank,
Fresh and free and frank;
Men of thought and reading,
Men of light and leading,
Men of loyal breeding,
The Nation's welfare speeding:

Men of faith and not of fiction,

Men of lofty aim and action;

Give us Men—I say again,

Give us Men!

Give us Men!

Strong and stalwart ones;

Men whom highest hope inspires,

Men whom purest honor fires,

Men who trample self beneath them,

Men who make their country wreathe them

As her noble sons,

Worthy of their sires;

Men who never shame their mothers,

Men who never fail their brothers,

True, however false are others:

Give us Men—I say again,

Give us Men!

Give us Men!

Men who, when the tempest gathers,

Grasp the Standard of their fathers

In the thickest fight:

Men who strike for home and altar,

(Let the coward cringe and falter,)

God defend the right!

True as truth though lorn and lonely,

Tender, as the brave are only;

Men who tread where saints have trod,

Men for Country, Home—and God:

Give us Men! I say again—again—

Give us such Men![1]

Why do men trade glory for boredom? Why do so many men fail to step up and become patriarchs? After pondering these questions, I identified the following reasons:

1. *Counterfeit manhood.* Many men didn't truly learn how to deny self and be real men when they had the opportunity to stand on the manhood step. Though they may know better now, they think it's too late to start being the men God has called them to be.

2. *The gender-blender lie.* Men can buy into the deception that the genders are the same, that there should be equal authority in the family. Therefore they think there is no unique calling or responsibility to be men in their later years.

3. *The lure of lesser loyalties.* Men embrace the modern-day notion that we work until we are sixty-five or seventy and then retire. They think they've earned the right to focus on enjoying life as they coast to the finish line.

4. *The loss of their chests.* Men are weary of the battle, of following God's call for their lives. They've lost heart as they look at a decaying culture, the problems in their families, or the number of health issues they face.

5. *Bitterness and cynicism.* As men grow old, they've experienced enough disappointment that they can easily become disillusioned, bitter, grumbly, and cynical. They can become crotchety old men. Note: you can't be a patriarch and crotchety at the same time.

Want to think about *Stepping Up* a little more or discuss it with your friends? Visit FamilyLife.com/Resources for a list of questions and talking points.

23
QUALITIES
OF A PATRIARCH

Without courage,
wisdom bears no fruit.
—BALTASAR GRACIAN,
SEVENTEENTH-CENTURY JESUIT PRIEST

A patriarch is a godly older man who, in his last season of life, has learned how to fight through his loss of authority and discover fresh ways of giving up his life on behalf of others. A powerful illustration of sacrificing one's life occurred in 1912 when the *Titanic* sank. Many men courageously remained on the boat so that women and children could be rescued.

Contrast the men of the *Titanic* with the cowards onboard an Indonesian vessel that sank in 1996. These men demanded preferential treatment and spots on the lifeboats over women and children. Does it feel manly, noble, and right that women and children should die so that men may live? These cowards lived while three hundred perished.

Author Douglas Phillips writes that one of the tenets of Christianity is that men are commanded by Scripture to sacrifice for their wives:

The groom dies for the bride, the strong suffer for the weak, and the highest expression of love is to give your life for another. This is the true meaning of biblical patriarchy. The men aboard the *Titanic* recognized their duty because they had been raised in a culture that implicitly embraced such notions.[1]

A man who aspires to be a patriarch has real vision—his physical eyesight may be failing him, but his generational vision has sharpened. The sage has 20/20 generational vision for his family, his community, and perhaps his nation. He understands that his family is in a generational relay race in which the lessons, values, and faith of one generation are being passed down to the generations that follow.

For more than a decade, I've studied the Bible to better understand what it says about this phase of a man's life. I've also talked to a couple dozen men and interviewed a number of adult children of fathers who were functioning as patriarchs. Three primary qualities have emerged from these conversations and my study.

1. A GENERATIONAL CONNECTOR

Patriarchs understand the power of love and relationships. True patriarchs are humble men of grace and forgiveness. They deliberately build relationships with their families.

The patriarchs I've interviewed were proactive in loving imperfect family members. They built relationships through organizing family reunions, keeping key family traditions alive, and encouraging communication between family members. Despite the challenges of being separated by hundreds of miles, they refused to allow relationships to grow cold.

Becoming a generational connector requires determination and perseverance. Yet the opportunities are endless:

- Determine to visit your adult children regularly, even if they live in other parts of the country. Go see them on "their turf" and don't just expect them to always come to your house.
- Take advantage of opportunities to babysit your grandchildren. Take one-on-one trips that build your relationship with them or pass on an important value. And as you spend time with your grandkids, be sure to tell them about your life and your faith.
- Consider organizing a yearly summer camp for your grandchildren. For nearly twenty years, Jerry and his wife, Patty, connected family members by hosting an annual "Cousins Camp." It was full of work, fun, and daily teaching—like a grandparent-run Vacation Bible School. In the process, Jerry was investing in the relationships of these little ones with him and with one another.
- Reach out to love and accept the spouses of your children. Send them notes and gifts. Express your appreciation for what they do for you. Encourage them during times of hardship. I know one dad who took his daughter-in-law on a shopping spree for some new clothes. Because of the home she grew up in, he sensed she needed an expression of a father's love. The impact on her life was powerful.

My father-in-law, Bob Peterson, is a patriarch. Married for more than sixty-three years, Bob is now in his late eighties and has been an incredible model to me of demonstrating love for his family. His consistent care for Donna, one of his daughters-in-law, was rewarded on his fiftieth wedding anniversary. As she read her tribute to Bob, it became evident that his love for her had a profound impact in her life.

Five of our six children are married, so I've had the privilege of welcoming five spouses into our family. I haven't done it as well as I'd wished, but one thing we've done is ask them to tell us their life stories. I'll never forget one evening sitting by a fire and listening as one of our daughters-in-law shared her story. I've taken all three of my sons-in-law hunting and to men's conferences with me. I've enjoyed getting to know two new daughters-in-law and trying to find ways to spoil them or let them know I'm thinking of them. I've written letters to them, gone shopping with them, and continued to pursue a relationship with each of them.

> ## PATRIARCHS AND THEIR WIVES ARE CRUCIAL TO KEEPING THEIR FAMILIES TOGETHER.

Patriarchs and their wives are crucial to keeping their families together. One friend likened his father's impact on his family's relationships to that of a linchpin; it wasn't until his dad's death that family members began to realize the real deposits of energy and leadership that he had invested to keep the family connected.

2. A GENERATIONAL INFLUENCER

The time and effort you put into connecting with your family may open the door for you to have an influence on them. The Scriptures teach that God has an assignment for every man (see Ephesians 2:10). Nowhere in the Bible does it say that these works cease at a certain age. No matter what our age, we are charged with stimulating others to love God with their whole heart and soul and might (see Deuteronomy 6:5–9).

As I mentioned earlier, one of the adjustments that a patriarch must face is that his authority changes. His children are directing their own families, and he no longer has the last word. In fact, he may not be asked for a "word." An effective patriarch learns that whatever power he has with others is that of influence.

Webster's defines *influence* as "the power or capacity of causing an effect in indirect or intangible ways." Influence can be wonderful. You can have an impact, but you don't have to carry the weight of being in charge.

Being a generational influencer means that you delight in seeing others excel. At this season of life, a patriarch doesn't have anything to prove. It's not about you; it's about those who are next. A courageous patriarch helps plant the seeds that others harvest. He delights in making an investment in a time beyond the horizon, investing in another generation. I'm reminded of what novelist Neil Postman wrote: "Children are the living messages we send to a time we will not see."

> A COURAGEOUS PATRIARCH HELPS
> PLANT THE SEEDS THAT OTHERS
> HARVEST. HE DELIGHTS IN MAKING
> AN INVESTMENT IN A TIME BEYOND
> THE HORIZON, INVESTING IN
> ANOTHER GENERATION.

One friend commented on relating to adult children: "I have learned that I must become smaller in my children's lives, not bigger." Become smaller by

- reminding your children of how big God is.
- bragging about your adult children to others, with them standing there.
- cheering on your adult children and other young men and women as they go through life. Use your words to bring life. Remember the proverb "Death and life are in the power of the tongue" (Proverbs 18:21).

- resigning as head coach, athletic director, and chancellor. Don't offer advice or opinions unless asked. This is so difficult when you see your children heading for a disaster. But zip it. Be small, very small.
- praising your children when they do something right. Make them big in the eyes of their spouses and children. Remember: we never outgrow our need for praise and appreciation.
- saying "I love you" often. I'm constantly amazed at how many men I meet who have never heard those words from their fathers. Kisses and hugs never hurt either.
- blessing your children and giving them your approval. Let them know you're proud of them—through your words and through handwritten notes and letters. I still have the last letter my dad wrote to me. I know a dad who is in the final weeks of his life, and his sons have never received his "blessing." Don't withhold some of the most important words that an older man can speak into the life of his son.

As I mentioned in the previous chapter, you can also be a generational influencer by passing on the family stories, "spiritual milestones" that speak of God's work on behalf of you and your family. These can be stories of answered prayers and of God's provision in tough times. Stories of how God has worked through you to touch lives. Consider writing some of these stories down and passing them on to your children and grandchildren.

I once interviewed a woman who had just returned from a family gathering. "My dad took the time to tell us how God has led and directed every part of his life," she said. "In a sense he gave us each a blessing. It was kind of like the Old Testament patriarchs."

Even in your final days, you can find ways to continue influencing your family. A powerful illustration of this is found in 1 Kings 2, where we find King David lying on his death bed, charging his son Solomon to be the man:

I am going the way of all the earth. Be strong, therefore, and show yourself a man. Keep the charge of the Lord your God, to walk in His ways, to keep His statutes, His commandments, His ordinances, and His testimonies, according to what is written in the Law of Moses, that you may succeed in all that you do and wherever you turn. (verses 2–3)

King David was standing on the patriarch step and reached down to his son to call him up to the next step. He commissioned his son to obey God and protect his heart and soul for his good, his family's good, and the good of the nation.

3. A GENERATIONAL INTERCESSOR

Perhaps the most strategic and effective way you can have an impact upon future generations is through prayer, your intercessory investments.

If God is truly almighty and in control—and He is; if prayer is talking with God—and it is; and if God hears and answers our prayers—and He does; then prayer is the most powerful tool we can use to be a connector and influencer in the lives of the next generation. The prayers of a patriarch beseech almighty God to do what only He can do—truly direct, protect, and change people's lives. The apostle James reminds us, "The effective prayer of a righteous man can accomplish much" (James 5:16).

Nearly every patriarch I interviewed mentioned this spiritual discipline as a part of his purpose in this stage of life. One man stated that prayer had become a new calling in his life. Another indicated that he would take a year and read the Bible all the way through with a child in mind, and pray for him or her. He would jot notes and prayers in the margins of a Bible for that child, and then at the end of the year, he would present the Bible to that child. Another mentioned how he spent time every day praying by name for each of his children and grandchildren and their impact on their world. And occasionally, as he prayed for them, he would send a text, e-mail, or letter to each child or grandchild, letting that child know he was praying for him or her.

I had the privilege of interviewing author Paul Miller about prayer. He gave me a very simple and yet profound way to pray for the needs of those we love the most. Paul uses a stack of three-by-five-inch cards, each with a name at the top. On the card he makes notes of specific ways to pray for his wife, children, and grandchildren. On the cards are specific character qualities and passages of Scripture that he prays for each person. Some of the cards he had in his stack were more than thirty years old.

I've been surprised as I've grown older at how often I find myself praying for my family, my community, and the world. I've always believed in prayer, but now I have fewer distractions and more time. I think one of the reasons prayer has become increasingly important is that I've come to realize that it really is my greatest contribution. In addition, I have the wisdom of a lifetime of knowing what my children need in their marriages, in raising their children, and in their careers. I've found that it's far more effective for me to talk to God about them than to talk to them about God.

AN IMPACT ON YOUR WORLD

As you step up to being a patriarch, recognize that God may give you the opportunity to use your experience and influence to have an impact beyond your family.

Dr. Carl Wenger had an enormous spiritual impact on his community. Dr. Wenger not only served the state of Arkansas as one of its most prominent surgeons; he also envisioned and ultimately created the Ozark Conference Center. Over the years this center has equipped thousands of young people and adults to be great citizens and wholehearted Christ followers.

Then in his eighties, I once asked Dr. Wenger, "What's the most important thing you've learned about being a patriarch?"

I've never forgotten his reply: "That God uses crooked sticks to draw straight lines."

As a man he was aware of his imperfections, brokenness, and need of a Savior. But that didn't stop him from being used to influence others for Christ.

Truett Cathy is another patriarch who is determined to influence his world. Mr. Cathy is the founder and CEO of Chick-fil-A, a nationwide fast-food business. His values demonstrate that you can make a living by working six days a week and taking Sunday off. Long after most men would have retired, Truett Cathy continues to invest in the next generation. His Win-Shape Foundation, for example, offers college scholarships, funds homes that provide long-term family care for children who are victims of circumstance, organizes summer camps, and helps couples learn how to enrich their marriages.

> "GOD USES CROOKED STICKS
> TO DRAW STRAIGHT LINES."

Perhaps you're at this season of life, considering "stepping up." Is it time for you to take advantage of your experience, time to have an influence on your world? You could teach younger men, husbands, and fathers. You could come alongside a younger leader in prayer. You could challenge other men of your age to become patriarchs. You could participate in mission trips in the States and overseas.

Will you step up?

Want to think about *Stepping Up* a little more or discuss it with your friends? Visit FamilyLife.com/Resources for a list of questions and talking points.

FINISHING WELL

It is nice to start well. It is even better to finish well.

—DR. WILLIAM CULBERTSON, FORMER PRESIDENT

OF MOODY BIBLE INSTITUTE

As an eight-year-old boy growing up in Hawaii, Bryan Clay dreamed of winning one of the most-prized gold medals in the Olympic Games—the decathlon. He accomplished that goal in Beijing in 2008.

In the decathlon, athletes earn points for their marks in ten events over two days. With a commanding lead going into the last event, the 1500-meter run, Clay could have assumed he could relax in the race and still earn the gold medal. But when Clay was asked when he knew that he had the decathlon title wrapped up, he surprised me with his reply:

In the last race when I was about 10 feet away from the finish line—
that's when I knew I'd won. I'd worked, trained and competed for
eight years to be able to stand on the top step and have the gold
hanging around my neck. And if there was anything those eight years
of competition had taught me it was that in competing against the

best in the world in ten grueling events, anything can go wrong before you cross the finish line.[1]

I've never competed in the Olympics, but I have competed in life. Like Bryan Clay, I've learned that the race isn't over until you cross the finish line. Even in the very last years of life—just short of the finish line—you can continue to be used by God. People still need you. You can still have an impact.

USED UP BY GOD

Consider the life of Dr. Oscar Remick, who spent nearly his entire life as a leader in educational institutions until he died at the age of sixty-nine when a rare cancer took his life in just seventeen days. He was known to say, "I want to be fully used up for the purposes of God. I want to live my life fully for Jesus Christ and expire."

"PEOPLE WERE DRAWN TO HIM. HIS TOTAL COMMITMENT WAS CONTAGIOUS."

A younger man he mentored named Scott described him: "He was 100 percent committed to being used by God for whatever, wherever. People were drawn to him. His total commitment was contagious."

We need models like Remick to show us how to live all the way to the end of life. My own father was only sixty-six when he died. I was twenty-eight at the time. Just as he was fully standing on the patriarch step, suddenly he was gone. As a young man, I had been robbed of the privilege of watching my dad grow old and gleaning lessons from his life. I needed an older man to show me what it looked like to finish well.

As I write these words, I am sixty-three and am acutely aware of how two older men have been a pair of divine gifts to me, giving me models of how to run these last laps of my life.

"PROF"

Dr. Howard Hendricks, affectionately known as "Prof," was the best teacher I sat under in more than eighteen years of academic studies. In one year I took all five of the classes he taught at Dallas Theological Seminary, and although he motivated me through the ceiling, he nearly killed me!

Prof didn't believe in tests; he believed in learning. That's why he loaded us up with homework every night. I was never so academically stretched in all my life.

Over a span of four decades, Prof and I became good friends. I taught him some of the nuances of fly-fishing, and he in turn taught me techniques in public speaking and communications. He created a hunger for truth in me and then taught me how to feed myself with the Scriptures. He continually expressed belief in me.

Prof gave me entire days when I came loaded with questions about loving my wife, raising children, and leading an organization. He took my calls. He and his wife, Jeanne, invested heavily by spending time with and mentoring the sixty couples who speak at our Weekend to Remember marriage getaways.

One of the most important things Prof taught and modeled was what the Bible had to say about aging. He "dusted my mind with itching powder" and taught me how to think about the last season of life. How to grow old with purpose instead of just growing old. How in God's economy, gray hairs are to be held in high esteem.

He modeled stretching out all the way to the finish line—teaching more than thirteen thousand students at Dallas Seminary over a span of sixty years, well into his eighties; discipling a dozen men in a small group; and keeping a vigorous speaking schedule long after he had a bout with cancer that took one of his eyes.

I'll never forget the day I heard that he had fallen and broken a couple of ribs. At the age of eighty-three, he had fallen off a platform at a conference where he'd been speaking. All because he had no sight in his right eye!

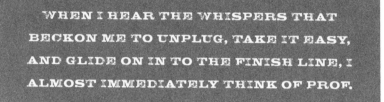

WHEN I HEAR THE WHISPERS THAT BECKON ME TO UNPLUG, TAKE IT EASY, AND GLIDE ON IN TO THE FINISH LINE, I ALMOST IMMEDIATELY THINK OF PROF.

Prof was like the Energizer Bunny—he just kept on going and going.

He showed me and thousands of others what it looks like to run well and finish well. When I hear the whispers that beckon me to unplug, take it easy, and glide on in to the finish line, I almost immediately think of Prof. I can't tell you what a motivation and source of strength his example was to me.

Prof's life led me to a profound conclusion: every man needs one or two older men in his life who model what it looks like to run with purpose all the way to the finish line and who finish well with smiles on their faces.

HE TAUGHT ME HOW TO LIVE AND HOW TO DIE

The other man God has used in my life was my boss for nearly thirty-five years—Dr. Bill Bright, founder and president of Campus Crusade for Christ.

For many years I considered Bill one of my mentors. He called himself a "bond slave" of Jesus Christ, and in so many ways, he taught me what it meant to be totally committed to Christ. He modeled how to trust in God no matter what I was feeling or experiencing. Watching Bill was better than an MBA in leadership.

He even kicked my tail on occasion. Early in my career, I made a presentation to him and asked for one million dollars. At the end he said nothing about my request but instead lectured me on at least a half-dozen grammatical errors I had made in my presentation! He cared enough to develop me as a young leader.

Once I came to him discouraged and asked if he had ever thought about quitting as a leader. He responded instantly with one word: "Never!" I thought he was kidding, but without blinking, he looked me square in the eye and calmly assured me, "I have never, ever, ever thought about quitting."

Bill taught me how to live, love, and lead, and in the last season of his life, how to die.

He was diagnosed with pulmonary fibrosis in the late 1990s and spent the next few years slowly losing the battle to breathe. He was on oxygen around the clock during the last couple of years, yet he modeled a purposeful, focused life all the way to the end. He reached out to encourage and exhort others. One time I visited him in the hospital, and he was working on a book, one of the eighty projects he had going at the time. He put his hand on mine, looked me in the eyes, and delegated one of those projects to me.

Later as I walked out of that hospital room, I realized what had happened. So I turned around and went back into his room with a big grin on my face and said to him, "Bill Bright, you are amazing. Here you are dying, and I came here to encourage you, and all you did was give me more work to do." I'll never forget him throwing both of his hands up in laughter.

Only a couple of months before his death, I had the privilege of interviewing Bill. That interview remains one of my top five out of more than three thousand interviews I've conducted over the past two decades.[2]

Bill continued working from his bed until his body began to shut down. He passed into heaven at the age of eighty-two to the sound of his family singing his favorite hymns. Bill Bright didn't rust out!

DON'T QUIT ON THE FINAL LAP

We all start the race that is set before us, but it is common for many of us to grow weary and lose heart along the way. It takes a courageous man to keep on keeping on. To keep on stepping up and to finish strong.

The Scriptures describe life as a race. In 1 Corinthians 9:24, Paul tells us, "Do you not know that those who run in a race all run, but only one receives the prize? Run in such a way that you may win." And Hebrews 12:1–3 says, "Let us run with endurance the race that is set before us, fixing our eyes on Jesus . . . so that you will not grow weary and lose heart."

You and I are in a race. Others are watching the direction we are running and how we are running. So run your race to win. And regardless where you find yourself on the steps of manhood today, I encourage you to do your duty—keep stepping up.

Though we can't choose the time we live in, we can, as Gandalf the Grey said in The Lord of the Rings, "decide what we do with the time that is given us."[3]

Want to think about *Stepping Up* a little more or discuss it with your friends? Visit FamilyLife.com/Resources for a list of questions and talking points.

IT'S TIME

A man's willingness to offer up his life for his wife or for
anybody else who happens to need him is not the end
of everything. It is only the end of himself. He who
is fully a man has relinquished his right to himself.

—ELISABETH ELLIOT,

The Mark of a Man

I have permission from Tim, my friend and the editor of *Stepping Up*, to tell one final story of a man stepping up courageously—Tim's story.

Now you should know that an editor and the author of a book can develop a very special relationship. Over the months of working together, they either really love and appreciate each other or they learn to merely tolerate each other. Or sometimes worse. But Tim and I have developed a mutual trust and appreciation, and as a result, we both have enjoyed the journey.

Tim is a credit to his craft. He's an excellent writer and editor. Our paths crossed four years ago as I was making my fourth unsuccessful pass at this book. He never lost the vision for this message. He became my coach and comrade, motivating and giving me encouragement that this book could and should be written. He is a good man.

Tim is also a big man.

He has shouldered a load that would have crushed lesser men when his wife died of ALS back in 1999, and he became the single parent of their four children, then ages four to thirteen. I marvel at what Tim has done, juggling the loss of his soul mate, handling the relentless demands of parenting solo, and excelling in his work. Tim has dreams of launching his children, enjoying grandchildren, and carving out more books of his own.

I have immense respect for Tim. And I am not alone in that opinion. But like all of us, Tim has his struggles—his weight being a perennial challenge. So as we worked on this book together and we developed a relationship of trust, it became clear to me that I needed to say something.

At the beginning of one of our last meetings, near the end of the editing process, I told Tim that I had two agenda items to discuss. The first was to determine the changes I needed to make to the book, and the second was something that had everything to do with the book *and* with him.

As we neared the end of our time, I transitioned to my second topic. I looked Tim in the eyes, paused, and was surprised at the emotion that filled my voice as I said two words to him: "It's time."

I didn't say anything else. Tim just looked at me, and after a few seconds of silence, he nodded and responded with two words: "I know."

There was another pause, and then he said with a smile, "I've been expecting this conversation. It *is* time."

That was three months ago. Tim is down thirty pounds as this book goes to press, with a goal of losing one hundred pounds by the end of the year. Two other friends, Bill and Steve, are checking in with Tim weekly and tracking his progress. I can't help but smile . . . between Bill and Steve's "tough love" and my sharing his story in a book about stepping up, well, let's just say Tim has more than a little accountability and a few more friends cheering him on.

You know, men, we really are in this thing called life together.

WHAT ABOUT YOU?

On this journey through the five steps, you've undoubtedly already stepped up and faced some issues. Some small issues, and perhaps some major ones. What I want you to do now is set an appointment for yourself to get alone for an hour, flip back through these pages, and ruthlessly ask yourself two questions:

1. Is there an issue in my life where it's become clear "It's time!"?
2. Is there a boy, a young man, a man, or a group of men in my life whom I need to give this book to? And maybe someday look them in the eye and say, "It's time"?

Whatever step you are straddling or standing on, may God give you the courage to step up and be His man.

Want to think about *Stepping Up* a little more or discuss it with your friends? Visit FamilyLife.com/Resources for a list of questions and talking points.

KNOWING GOD
PERSONALLY

Faith is taking the first step
even though you don't see
the whole staircase.

—MARTIN LUTHER KING JR.

If you want to take the ultimate step up and experience life the way God designed it, then you need a relationship with Him. If you want to live as the man God intended you to be, then you need to know the God who created you.

Our problem is that because of pride, we have rejected God's authority in our lives and have chosen to go our own way. Our sin separates us from Him. Though we may try to earn God's approval and deal with our sin by working hard to become better people, we must understand that the problem of sin runs much deeper than bad habits and will take more than our best behavior to overcome. God's Word clearly tells us that we cannot close the gap between ourselves and God on our own:

All of us like sheep have gone astray,
each of us has turned to his own way. (Isaiah 53:6)

There is a way that seems right to a man,
but its end is the way to death. (Proverbs 14:12)

The wages of sin is death. (Romans 6:23)

God is holy, and we are sinful. No matter how hard we try, we cannot come up with some plan, such as living a good life or trying to do what the Bible says, and hope that we can be "good enough" to earn a relationship with God.

The bottom line: our sin separates us from God. We need a Savior.

GOD'S INVITATION

Thankfully, God has provided the way to solve our dilemma. He became a man in the person of Jesus Christ. Jesus lived a holy life in perfect obedience to God and willingly died on a cross to pay the penalty for our sin. Then He proved that He is more powerful than sin or death by rising from the dead.

Jesus said to [Thomas], "I am the way, and the truth, and the life;
no one comes to the Father but through Me." (John 14:6)

God demonstrates His own love toward us, in that while we were yet
sinners, Christ died for us. (Romans 5:8)

The wages of sin is death, but the free gift of God is eternal life in Christ
Jesus our Lord. (Romans 6:23)

For I delivered to you as of first importance what I also received, that
Christ died for our sins according to the Scriptures, and that He was
buried, and that He was raised on the third day according to the
Scriptures, and that He appeared to Cephas, then to the twelve. After
that He appeared to more than five hundred brethren at one time.
(1 Corinthians 15:3–6)

The life, death, and resurrection of Jesus have provided the way to establish a relationship between you and God.

ACCEPTING GOD'S INVITATION

When the Bible talks about receiving Christ, it means we acknowledge that we can't save ourselves from the penalty or the power of sin. Receiving Christ means that we repent, or turn away from, our sin and trust Christ to forgive our sins and make us the kind of people He wants us to be. It's not enough to just intellectually acknowledge that Christ is the Son of God. As an act of the will, we must place our faith and trust in Him and surrender our lives to Him and His plan for us:

For by grace you have been saved through faith; and that not of your-
selves, it is the gift of God; not a result of works, so that no one may
boast. (Ephesians 2:8–9)

When we accept the incredible gift God offers us, we become His children:

But as many as received Him, to them He gave the right to become
children of God, even to those who believe in His name. (John 1:12)

Are things right between you and God? Is He the center of your life? Is His plan for your life the priority of your life? Or is life spinning out of control as you seek to go your own way?

If you have been going your own way, you can decide today to ask Him to forgive all your sins and begin the process of changing you. You can turn to Christ, surrender your life to Him, and begin the adventure of allowing Jesus Christ and the Scriptures to transform your life. All you need to do is talk to Him in faith and tell Him what is stirring in your mind and heart.

Prayer may be new to you, but understand that God knows your heart and is not so concerned with your words as He is with the attitude of your heart. Here is a suggested prayer to guide you:

> *Lord Jesus, I need You. Thank You for dying on the cross for my sins. I receive You as my Savior and Lord. Thank You for forgiving my sins and giving me eternal life. Make me the kind of person You want me to be. Amen.*

If you prayed this prayer, or if you still have questions about knowing God personally, please visit the website MatthiasMedia.com.au/2wtl.

Chapter 1

1. The story of Eugene "Red" Erwin is retold by the author based on the information found in "Master Sgt. Henry E. 'Red' Erwin," Air Force Enlisted Heritage Institute, http://www.af.mil/information/heritage/person.asp?dec=&pid=123006484; and John L. Frisbee, "Red Erwin's Personal Purgatory," *Air Force Magazine* 72, no. 10 (October 1989), http://www.airforce-magazine.com/Magazine Archive/Pages/1989/October%201989/1089valor.aspx.

Chapter 3

1. John Piper, *What's the Difference: Manhood and Womanhood Defined According to the Bible* (Wheaton, IL: Crossway Books, 1990), 19.

2. Peggy Noonan, "Welcome Back, Duke," Opinion Journal, *Wall Street Journal*, October 12, 2001.

Chapter 4

1. Steve Vogel, "Tomb Guards Stand Sentinel Through Isabel's Threatening Sweep," *Washington Post*, October 2, 2003.

2. Data from Natality Data Sets, National Vital Statistics System, cited in Stephanie J. Ventura, "Changing Patterns of Nonmarital Childbearing in the United States," *National Center for Health Statistics Data Brief*, no. 18 (May 2009).

3. U.S. Census Bureau Current Population Survey, reported in "Living Arrangements of Children in the United States over Time," National Healthy Marriage Resource Center, accessed December 15, 2010, www.healthymarriageinfo.org.

4. David Blankenhorn, *Fatherless America: Confronting Our Most Urgent Social Problem* (New York: HarperPerennial, 1996), 49.

5. Crawford Loritts, *Leadership as an Identity: The Four Traits of Those Who Wield Lasting Influence* (Chicago: Moody Publishers, 2009), 185.

6. Adapted from John Piper and Wayne Grudem, eds., *Recovering Biblical Manhood and Womanhood: A Response to Evangelical Feminism* (Wheaton, IL: Crossway Books, 2006), 43.

Chapter 5

1. The story is retold by the author based on the information found in Jeff Rennicke, "Father Kills Bear to Save Son," *Reader's Digest* (September 2009), http://www.rd.com/your-america-inspiring-people-and-stories/father-kills-bear-to-save-son/article156354.html; Ron Leming Jr., "Backcountry Grizzly Attack," *Outdoor Life*, October 28, 2008, http://www.outdoorlife.com/photos/gallery/survival/2008/10/backcountry-grizzly-attack?photo=0#node-1000 022973; and Brett French, "Life-Saving Bow Shot Downs Grizzly Bear," *Billings Gazette*, October 16, 2008, http://helenair.com/lifestyles/recreation/article_57124e03-16fb-5306-ae58-c5a04f 5f9235.html.

2. Rennicke, "Father Kills Bear."

3. Ibid.

4. Leming, "Backcountry Grizzly Attack."

5. Rennicke, "Father Kills Bear."

6. Ibid.

7. French, "Life-Saving Bow Shot."

8. Rennicke, "Father Kills Bear."

9. French, "Life-Saving Bow Shot."

10. Rennicke, "Father Kills Bear."

Chapter 6

1. Peg Tyre, "The Trouble with Boys," *Newsweek*, January 30, 2006, http://www.newsweek.com/2006/01/29/the-trouble-with-boys .html.

2. Jacqueline E. King, *Gender Equity in Higher Education: 2006* (Washington, DC: American Council on Education, 2010).

3. Tyre, "The Trouble with Boys."

Chapter 8

1. Edgar Guest, *Between You and Me: My Philosophy of Life* (Chicago: Reilly and Lee, 1938), 229–32.

2. Joshua Wooden, as cited in John Wooden and Jay Carty, *Coach Wooden One-On-One* (Ventura, CA: Gospel Light, 2003), 38.

3. Lee Fisher, "A Little Fellow Follows Me," as cited in Wooden and Carty, *Coach Wooden*.

Chapter 9

1. The account of Winston Churchill is taken from William Manchester, *The Last Lion: Winston Spencer Churchill: Alone 1932– 1940* (Boston: Little, Brown, 1988); Martin Gilbert, *Churchill: A Life* (New York: Henry Holt, 1991); and Winston S. Churchill, *Never Give In! The Best of Winston Churchill's Speeches* (New York: Hyperion Books, 2003).

2. Winston Churchill, cited in Manchester, *The Last Lion*, 70.

3. Ibid.

4. Lady Astor, cited in *The Last Lion*, 85.

5. Ibid., 86.

6. Ibid., 20.

7. Reporter, cited in *The Last Lion*, 88.

8. Churchill, *Never Give In!* 206.

Chapter 10

1. Alex Harris, "The Myth of Adolescence," *The Rebelution* (blog), August 19, 2005, accessed December 15, 2010, http://www .therebelution.com/2005/08/myth-of-adolescence-part-1.html.
2. Michael Kimmel, *Guyland: The Perilous World Where Boys Become Men* (New York: HarperCollins, 2008), 4.

Chapter 11

1. Adapted from Dennis Rainey and Barbara Rainey, *Parenting Today's Adolescent: Helping Your Child Avoid the Traps of the Preteen and Teen Years* (Nashville: Thomas Nelson, 1998), 3–4. All rights reserved. Used by permission.

Chapter 12

1. The Fred Stoeker story is taken from "Equipping Your Son for Every Man's Battle," interview by Dennis Rainey and Bob Lepine, *FamilyLife Today* (November 15, 2004). All rights reserved. Used by permission.
2. In *Every Man's Battle* (WaterBrook, 2000), Fred Stoeker describes his own slide into sexual immorality. His experience with pornography as a boy shows the importance of a father's protective involvement.

Chapter 13

1. The account of Ernest Shackleton's Antarctic expedition was taken from Caroline Alexander, *The Endurance* (New York: Knopf, 1999); Sir Ernest Shackleton, *South!* (New York: Macmillan, 1920); and F. A. Worsley, *Endurance* (New York: W. W. Norton, 1931).
2. Alexander, *The Endurance*, 44.
3. Shackleton, *South!* 96.

4. Ibid., 177.

5. Worsley, *Endurance*, 156.

6. Shackleton, *South!* 203.

7. Ibid., 124.

8. University of Colorado Boulder Institute of Arctic and Alpine Research, *Arctic and Alpine Research* 18 (Boulder: University of Colorado, 1986).

Chapter 15

1. My book *Interviewing Your Daughter's Date* offers practical advice for parents who are committed to protecting and guiding their daughters through the dating years. For more information, see http://www.shopfamilylife.com/interviewing-your-daughters-date.html.

Chapter 17

1. A. W. Tozer, *The Knowledge of the Holy* (New York: HarperCollins, 1985), 1.

Chapter 18

1. The account of Jackie Robinson was taken from Jackie Robinson, as told to Alfred Duckett, *I Never Had It Made* (New York: Putnam, 1972); Jonathan Eig, *Opening Day: The Story of Jackie Robinson's First Season* (New York: Simon and Schuster, 2007); and Arnold Rampersad, *Jackie Robinson: A Biography* (New York: Ballantine, 1997), 186–87.

2. Robinson, *I Never Had It Made*, 25.

3. Ibid., 33–34.

4. Eig, *Opening Day*, 45.

5. Robinson, *I Never Had It Made*, 59.

6. Eig, *Opening Day*, 107.

7. Ibid., 222–23.

8. Rampersad, *Jackie Robinson*, 186–87.

Chapter 19

1. Mary Anne Radmacher, *Courage Doesn't Always Roar* (San Francisco: Conari Press, 2009), dedication.

Chapter 21

1. The account of Beck Weathers was taken from Beck Weathers with Stephen G. Michaud, *Left for Dead* (New York: Villard Books, 2000); and Jon Krakauer, *Into Thin Air* (New York: Villard Books, 1997). The quote in this paragraph is from *Left for Dead*, 50.

2. Weathers, *Left for Dead*, 52.

3. Ibid., 42–43.

4. Krakauer, *Into Thin Air*, 108.

5. Ibid., 247.

6. Ibid., 248.

7. Weathers, *Left for Dead*, 7.

8. Ibid., 52.

9. Ibid., 53.

10. Ibid., 54.

11. Ibid., 58.

12. Ibid., 60.

13. "About Beck Weathers MD," Keppler Speakers, accessed December 17, 2010, http://www.kepplerspeakers.com/speakers.aspx?name= Beck+Weathers,+MD.

Chapter 22

1. Bishop of Exeter, "Give Us Men!" public domain, cited in John

Phillips Meakin, comp., *From the Four Winds* (Rahway, NJ: Quinn and Boden, 1911), 7–8.

Chapter 23

1. Douglas W. Phillips, "Titanic Chivalry," *World Magazine* 13, no. 12 (March 28, 1998): 29.

Chapter 24

1. Bryan Clay, personal interview by Jim Campbell, February 2009, National Religious Broadcaster's Convention, Nashville, TN.
2. You can listen to the *FamilyLife Today* interview with Bill Bright, titled "Finish the Race," day 2 in Reflections of Life: A Personal Visit with Bill Bright (May 21, 2009) at http://www.familylife.com/site/apps/nlnet/content3.aspx?c=dnJHKLNnFoG&b=3781631&ct=6962137.
3. J. R. R. Tolkien, *The Fellowship of the Ring*, 2nd ed. (Boston: Houghton Mifflin, 1965), 60.

ABOUT THE AUTHOR

Dennis Rainey is the president and CEO of FamilyLife (a ministry of Cru) and a graduate of Dallas Theological Seminary. For more than thirty-five years, he has been speaking and writing on marriage and family issues. Since 1976, he has overseen the development of FamilyLife's numerous outreaches, including the popular Weekend to Remember marriage getaway. He is also the daily host of the nationally syndicated radio program *FamilyLife Today*®. He and his wife, Barbara, reside in Little Rock, Arkansas, and have six adult children and numerous grandchildren.

CONNECT WITH AUTHOR

 @DennisRainey

facebook.com/raineydennis

Get away with
your teenager for an
adventure of a lifetime!

Your teen begins the journey into adulthood into a world of questions and a multitude of voices. His identity is under attack. You cannot win the battle with a single awkward talk or a strict set of rules. FamilyLife's Passport2Identity (P2I) will guide you in building heart-to-heart communication with your teen while laying a foundation of identity that will prepare him for the critical years ahead.

The Passport2Identity Getaway Kit includes

- tour guide for the parent;
- travel journal for the teen including 25 follow-up devotions; and
- 8 CDs containing 5 sessions, Scripture memory songs and downloadable MP3s.

1-800-FL-Today
www.Passport2Identity.com
(recommended ages 14–16)

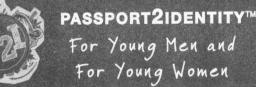

PASSPORT2IDENTITY™
For Young Men and
For Young Women

Get away with
your pre-teen for an
adventure of a lifetime!

Passport2Purity® will guide you and your pre-teen through biblical principles regarding peer pressure, dating and sex. Dennis and Barbara Rainey will lead you through this one-on-one retreat with your son or daughter. It's a great time full of discovery, communication and fun.

PASSPORT2PURITY®
1-800-FL-TODAY • Passport2Purity.com
(recommended ages 9–12)

FAMILYLIFE® presents
weekend to remember®

GREAT MARRIAGES

DON'T JUST

happen.

Wouldn't it be great if "happily ever after" really were the end of the story?
Great marriages require intentionality and investment—just like a garden that must be watered in order to grow. Weekend to Remember is a two-and-a-half day weekend getaway that offers:

- biblically-based insights from top speakers and marriage experts;
- relaxing time alone together, free from distractions; and
- helpful tools and resources for an immediate impact on your marriage.

Get intentional about taking your marriage to the next level.

SAVE $100 per couple.
Go to WeekendtoRemember.com or call
1-800-FL-TODAY and use group code FLPFRIENDS.

TODAY, MORE THAN EVER, THE WORLD NEEDS GODLY MEN...

... men who will step up and courageously lead at home, at church, at work, and in their communities.

That's where Stepping Up™ comes in. Stepping Up gives men the tools they need to make a difference in today's world—through high-quality DVDs that feature engaging stories, humorous vignettes, interviews, and personal insights from many of today's ministry leaders, including Dennis Rainey, Matt Chandler, Tony Dungy, and Voddie Baucham.

One-day Video Event

Designed for a momentum-building single-day event or weekend retreat, Dennis Rainey hosts the four sessions that focus on defining manhood, living courageously, building a life of faith, and stepping up to lead.

10-week Video Series

Expanded study lets men dig deeper into what is means to step up. Twenty-two ministry leaders unpack what biblical manhood looks like and what it means to be a godly, courageous man in today's world.

Book

Dennis Rainey connects at the heart level and challenges men at each step in life's journey to reject passivity and embrace courage. Available in hardcover, audio, and e-book formats.

What others are saying:

"The truth was presented in a way that convicted, encouraged, and challenged me."

"This was probably the most impactful men's event I have been to. Its lessons will stick with me for a long time."

Learn more at **FamilyLife.com/SteppingUp**